PALM SPRINGS
AND THE COACHELLA VALLEY

TEXT AND PHOTOGRAPHS BY
JIM CARR

AMERICAN GEOGRAPHIC PUBLISHING

American Geographic Publishing is a corporation for publishing illustrated geographic information and guides. It is not associated with American Geographical Society. It has no commercial or legal relationship to and should not be confused with any other company, society or group using the words geographic or geographical in its name or its publications.

ISBN 0-938314-68-8

text © 1989 Jim Carr
© 1989 American Geographic Publishing
P.O. Box 5630, Helena, MT 59604
(406) 443-2842

William A. Cordingley, Chairman
Rick Graetz, Publisher & CEO
Mark O. Thompson
  Director of Publications
Barbara Fifer, Production Manager

Design by Len Visual Design

Printed in Hong Kong

Above and right: *Desert Horizon Resort at Indian Wells.* JIM CARR
Title page: GEORGE SERVICE

Cover photographs: *Landscape and palm-leaf background:* GEORGE SERVICE
License plate and back cover: JIM CARR

To my wife

and best friend,

Helen, because...

Jim Carr is a photojournalist whose work has been published in *Palm Springs Life, Today's Secretary, Science News, Advertising Age, New Jersey Business, Focus, Family Digest* and many other periodicals. He has written hundreds of feature articles for newspapers throughout the United States. His photography has been purchased by several corporations and publications and is represented by The Travel Image, a stock photography source.

For 25 years, Carr administered corporate communications for leading companies, including Xerox Corporation and Litton Industries, before turning full time to photojournalism. His freelance work has taken him to Europe, Africa, the Arctic and the Orient, as well as to many North American locations. He lives with his wife, Helen, in Cathedral Canyon Country Club in Cathedral City, California.

A former newspaper reporter and radio news director, Carr was an Air Force air traffic controller before graduating from St. Bonaventure University and teaching at the Boston University Graduate School of Journalism. He is a member of the Society of Professional Journalists, American Society of Magazine Photographers and the Desert Press Club.

George Service, whose photography appears throughout the book, has been photographing nature subjects in the desert for the past 25 years. He specializes in the American southwestern deserts and Baja California, noting that "each desert is a distinct world unto itself, particularly botanically." His work has appeared in *Audubon, Nature Conservancy* and other natural history publications, and has been exhibited at the Palm Springs Desert Museum and the Living Desert.

AUTHOR'S NOTE

Historical information in this book has come from many, many sources including community histories, personal memories, convention bureaus, merchants, writers and town and city leaders. I think—and hope—most of it is accurate. If a boo-boo sneaked in here and there, I apologize...but with or without them, the story needed telling.

CONTENTS

Above: Spring-break traffic on Palm Canyon Drive.

A NATURAL WONDER

CHAPTER ONE

Home to 200,000 and host

to millions annually, the

valley has many extremes.

The wonder of California's Palm Springs desert resort area isn't its climate, celebrities or golf courses, as great as they are. The wonder is that it *exists at all!*

Many thousand years ago, after earthquakes ringed the Coachella Valley with majestic mountains, the area became a finger of the Gulf of California. Early Indians tilled the foothills and fished the ancient shores. Eventually, sealed off from the sea by an expanding Colorado River delta, the remaining waters evaporated and the region became a salty spot in the great American desert.

Bounded on the north and east by the Little San Bernardino Mountains, with Mount San Jacinto and San Gorgonio Mountain to the west, and the Santa Rosa Mountains and the Salton Sea to the south, the Coachella Valley today is home to 200,000 and host to millions annually.

Right: Seventeen Palms Oasis in Anza-Borrego State Park.
Above: Beavertail cactus blooms in Palm Desert. GEORGE SERVICE PHOTOS

6

A region of extremes in geography, temperatures, wealth and lifestyles, this ritzy resort area sprang from a wasteland little more than a century ago to become a world-renowned cluster of tourist attractions.

"The key to Palm Springs' existence," writes author Peter Benchley, "is…climate!" Indeed, the weather in the Coachella Valley is probably the most consistently predictable of any place on the continent.

Sunshine warms the desert sands all year. Mid-day temperatures hover between 60 and 90 degrees, most of the time. And even in summer, when the mercury can rocket up to 115 degrees and more, the humidity normally remains a comfortable 20 percent.

Light early-morning frosts in January and February bring sweater weather—and some short delays in the tee times on the valley's more than 70 golf courses. But the year-round average daytime high is about 88 degrees, the nighttime average is a comfortable 55 degrees. So, for the leading hassle-free job, the local weather forecasters vie only with TV's Maytag repairman.

Yes, it actually does rain here in the desert—but not often. The average of 15 to 20 rain days each year in the Palm Springs area prompted one local car-wash to offer a free return if the first cleaning got rained on that day.

But when rain does come to the Coachella Valley, it often brings with it spectacular rainbows. Like celestial laser lights, these multihued displays fill the valley and ring the nearby mountains. More often the lower desert appears to be no more than a barren expanse of blowing sand. But time and rain change all that. In 1987, several acres of desert verbena carpeted a field on Bob Hope Drive in Rancho Mirage. Two years later, lack of winter rain produced a field of—nothing. But with the next winter of sufficient moisture, the field may again bloom in profusion—once or maybe twice! The desert is in no hurry. It can wait.

Showiest of all Coachella Valley cacti is the beaver-tail. Early each spring, this Sonoran Desert native bursts forth with stunning magenta or yellow blossoms. When nurtured by late rain, the beaver-tails fill the region with intense color. While this cactus will grow at elevations up to 4,000 feet, it gives its best performance on the heated desert floor. (But a warning! Those cute little tufts on the beaver-tail that appear pussy-willow-soft hide needle-sharp spines that give a nasty punch.)

The name and nature of the region are, of course, its ubiquitous palm trees. No one seems able to determine exactly how many palms are now in the Coachella Valley. There are more than 3,000 in Palm Canyon and an estimated 10,000 in the city of Palm Springs alone. In addition, there are some 40 palm oases scattered across the valley. And every country club, estate and yard seems to be fully palm-tree shaded.

Through the efforts of Ruth Hardy, Palm Springs' first city councilwoman, some 1,200 Washingtonia palms were planted as a grand corridor along the city's Palm Canyon Drive in the 1960s. Native to

8

Above: Gambrel quail at Living Desert in Palm Desert.
Facing page: San Jacinto after a winter storm in December—a view from Whitewater.
GEORGE SERVICE PHOTOS BOTH PAGES

Joshua Tree National Monument after a winter storm.

California, Arizona and Mexico, the Washingtonia palm frequently is planted in the valley. They grow naturally near springs and thrive in the desert heat. Their fan-shaped foliage stands on long stems in open crowns. The *robusta*, or "Mexican fan palm," version of the Washingtonia has a tall, slender trunk; the fatter, short-trunked version is the "California fan palm," called *filifera*.

Northeast of the valley, the palm oases give way to the sharp rise of the Little San Bernardino Mountains, which contain the unusual Joshua Tree National Monument. This half-million-acre reserve was established in 1936 at the intersection of the Mojave (high) and Colorado (low) deserts.

Gnarled and oddly twisted branches of the Joshua tree brought the plant its name. Mormon pioneers thought it resembled the Biblical prophet, Joshua, welcoming travelers to the Promised Land. Actually, the Joshua tree is a giant yucca plant, which can reach 30 feet high and display splendid cream-white blossoms in spring.

While the land in the monument may appear dead and deserted, it actually contains delicate and intricate living systems, each depending on the others for survival. And the granite monoliths and twisted rock found in the monument bear mute testimony to the volcanic pressures that formed the area. In summer, wild flowers in a rainbow of color cover the ground. But, in winter, snow often brings the scene an eerie blanket of white. As dismal as this desert rim may appear, life-forms are here in abundance. Golden eagles soar in the sun and, by night, tarantulas, lizards and coyotes roam. From bobcats to burrowing owls and yucca night lizards to strange little black "stinkbugs" that do head stands when disturbed, the desert is, indeed, alive. As one sign urges visitors: "Stand and look at the desert around you for a few minutes. What looks deserted is really alive." But, the desert, fascinating as it is, can be unforgiving to those unfamiliar with its potential dangers.

In 1873, gold was discovered here and visitors today still can roam the Lost Horse, Desert Queen and Golden Bee mines. Key's View, a Joshua Tree lookout point more than 5,000 feet above sea level, offers a panoramic view of the Coachella Valley and one of its best-kept secrets, Lake Cahuilla, nestled in the foothills of the Santa Rosa mountains.

Once upon a time, according to Indian lore, an ancient Lake Cahuilla had covered the entire valley. When it receded to the ocean, some 500 years ago, it left tiny seashells—*conchellas*—as far as 1,000 feet up the hillsides. It's thought the valley's modern name, Coachella, may have come from a map maker's error in spelling this old Spanish word. The original lake's high-water marks still can be seen in the travertine rock rimming the mountainsides. Built in 1969, the "new" Lake Cahuilla is a man-made terminus of the All American Canal. Almost a mile long and half that wide, the lake has become a central recreation site and is stocked with bass and catfish in summer and trout in winter.

Top right: *Great horned owl at Living Desert in Palm Desert.*
Bottom: *Red diamondback at elevation of 1,500 feet in Santa Rosa Mountains.*
GEORGE SERVICE PHOTOS BOTH PAGES

11

Hidden away from valley view are the five lush Indian Canyons, still owned by the Cahuilla people.

Mythologically, the portals of paradise were ever guarded by brooding, muscled denizens of the dark to ensure the felicity of the residents. The Coachella Valley communities, strung like jewels along Highway 111, have their own set of protectors who warily observe those daring to traverse the Banning Pass, western gateway to the resort region.

Soaring almost two miles high on either side of the often wind-whipped pass are the twin peaks of San Gorgonio Mountain on the north and Mount San Jacinto opposite—the highest summits in southern California. A natural northwestern boundary, these rocky sentinels do, indeed, protect their domain—especially against the unwelcome wave of smog pushing eastward from the Los Angeles basin, 100 miles to the west.

Interstate 10, the Christopher Columbus Highway, snakes its way between these mighty mountains into the Salton Trough, a 2,000-square-mile ditch that dives to 273 feet below sea level. In the United States, only Death Valley, which covers a lesser area, is slightly deeper at minus 282 feet.

About October of each year, as most North American cities begin to hunker down for a frigid winter, the Coachella Valley unfurls the welcome signs and gears up for what locals call "The Season." From then until the last student leaves bleary-eyed from a boisterous Easter vacation, it will play warm-weather host to the world's "snowbirds."

Stretching southeast across the valley, the desert resort cities include Palm Springs, Cathedral City, Rancho Mirage, Palm Desert, Indian Wells, La Quinta and Indio. Farther down the valley are Thermal, Oasis and Mecca, the agricultural heart of the area. Desert Hot Springs lies north of Interstate 10, just a few miles from Palm Springs. Collectively, these communities offer more than 15,000 hotel rooms, with 6,000 more in planning or construction. In Palm Springs, however, even if you park in front of your room, you are never in a "motel"—only hotels, inns, casas, spas, apartments, villas or clubs are your hosts!

While each of the desert resort communities maintains a separate

Moonlight turns the Coachella Valley into a sparkling wonderland. View from Bob Hope's Palm Springs home.

GEORGE SERVICE

Top: Derelict farming equipment still can be found in the former desert grazing area in North Palm Springs.
Above: Sandy beach and clear blue water welcome guests at the valley's newest hotel, Stouffer's Esmeralda in Indian Wells.
Right: Palm Canyon winds 15 miles from its visitor center and gift shop into the mountains.

13

A region of extremes in geography, temperatures, wealth and lifestyles, this ritzy resort area sprang from a wasteland little more than a century ago to become a world-renowned cluster of tourist attractions.

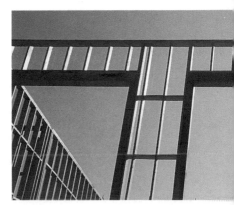

Left: *Hiking in Palm Canyon can be as easy or strenuous as you wish, from rocky slopes to well worn trails.*
Above: *New construction in all parts of the desert resort area is geared to the needs of a doubling population.*
Top: *Casa Cody in Palm Springs is a fine example of the many small hotels throughout the desert resort area.*

Facing page: *Verdant fairways at The Lakes Country Club in Palm Desert are among the more than 70 courses in the Coachella Valley.*

15

If the Salton Sea seems

oddly out of place, it

should—it's the result of a

1905 construction error by

railroad workers building a

Colorado River crossing.

identity, visitors usually refer to the entire resort area as Palm Springs—much to the chagrin of the newer and faster-growing communities.

Hidden from valley view are the Indian Canyons, settled centuries ago by the Cahuilla Indian Tribe. Like the imprint of a giant hand, the five canyons cut into the mountain's edge on the valley's southern side.

Named Palm, Andreas, Murray, Chino and Tahquitz, these lush cuts curve through craggy rock and icy mountain streams. Chino is home of the Palm Springs Aerial Tramway and only Tahquitz requires a special visitor's permit. Visitors to the trails and shady picnic grounds of the Murray and Andreas canyons are reminded what life was like here before white settlers arrived.

Palm Canyon boasts more than 3,000 desert fan palms, the largest fan oasis in the world. This canyon winds calmly some 15 miles and still is owned and maintained by the Indians. A magnet for hikers, Palm Canyon suffered a severe fire a decade ago. Many blackened trunks can be found on the 75-foot palms, which regenerate even after facing such scorching flames.

Known to early Indians and Spanish explorers as "La Palma de la Mano de Dios" (The Hollow of God's Hand), this tranquil palm patch remains an oasis just minutes from the burgeoning valley development and traffic.

A one-hour drive and a mile above the canyons via the Palms to Pines Highway (Route 74 south from Palm Desert) is Idyllwild. This Alpine-styled village is within hiking distance of Tahquitz Peak, which at almost 9,000 feet brings not only a cool respite from the sandy desert heat but also panoramic views of the valley floor and the Salton Sea.

In winter, if the snow is sufficient, sled dog races are held between Idyllwild and the top of the tramway. During summer, workshops at the 30-year-old ISOMATA (The Idyllwild School of Music and the Arts) attract students from around the world to its conference center.

From Idyllwild, the 35-mile-long Salton Sea appears to be a wondrous joke of nature. Sparkling turquoise under some skies, and muddy dark under others, this sea is ringed by chocolate-colored mountains.

Somehow, this enormous foot-print in the sand seems oddly out of place. And well it should! For this salty moat guarding the Coachella Valley's southern flank was the result of a man-made error.

In 1905, workers on a proposed rail crossing of the Colorado River miscalculated the power of "Big Red." The river surged against a weakened levee causing a disastrous half-mile break. More than 4 million cubic feet of water per day roared into the huge salt marsh remaining from the area's oceanic origins. So extensive were these early salty deposits that even today this inland sea is saltier than the ocean.

After more than two years, the flow was stemmed. But by then, more than 50 miles of railroad track was gone and the new Imperial Salt Company plant looked up from under 60 feet of water.

Above: Snowy egret at bird sanctuary at Salton Sea.
Facing page: Sand verbena in Palm Desert.
GEORGE SERVICE PHOTOS BOTH PAGES

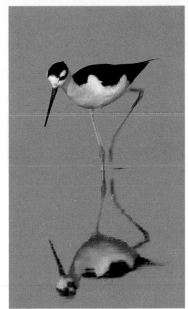

ABOVE AND FACING PAGE: GEORGE
SERVICE PHOTOS

"Big Red" was finally brought under control with the completion of Hoover Dam on the Arizona-Nevada border. Today the All American Canal System feeds water to some half million acres in the Imperial and Coachella valleys, some of the richest and most productive irrigated farmland in the world.

A grand resort for migratory aquatic birds, the saline lake offers great food and facilities for birds. It is an essential link along the Pacific flyway. Snowy egrets, great blue herons and honking geese stop here each year by the thousands. Some 75 species make their year-round homes there, while 350 other species drop in for the winter. These are the true "snowbirds." Almost one third of all North American white pelicans set up nest-keeping there, about the time human tourists start their annual trek to the desert resort area.

The extreme salt level of the Salton Sea causes strange phenomena. Today the sea has ironwood trees that sink and pumice rocks that float. The sea's surface is about 250 feet below sea level and its average depth is a mere 10 to 12 feet most of the year. A haven for fishermen seeking the elusive corvina, this shimmering sea can be deceptively dangerous for those caught out on it during the sudden sand and wind storms that often occur.

Like most of the planet today, the Salton Sea is facing environmental problems. It is troubled by industrial waste, sewage and agricultural runoff. These affect not only the fish, but also the birds that feed on them.

Salinity levels seem to be rising. This cuts back spawning of the resident sport fish. And now changing percentages of selenium have prompted warnings against eating certain amounts of local fish.

Several plans currently are being weighed to ensure the sea's future. One suggests using the sea's salty residue to produce solar energy; another calls for a 50-mile dike to improve the reduced area with new inflowing water. Yet a third thought is to connect the Salton Sea with the Gulf of California in hopes the merging waters would lower the salt level. Costs of such plans are estimated to range from $140 to $350 million over a five- to 10-year period.

Strong winds also rake the western end of the valley. There, however, they have been tamed and put to use.

Ancient Indians told of the demon "Tahquitz" who inhabited the western hills and, when displeased, caused wild winds and severe celestial disturbances. Today, modern technology has replaced this mythical spirit with more than 4,000 of its own "totem" poles, which generate an even greater power.

Since 1983, these wind turbines rising 80 feet in the air have sprouted in the passes east of Cabazon. While the first turbines generated little more than 20 kilowatts of electricity apiece, newer models now under construction are capable of 500 kilowatts each. Last year, this wind farm

Top right: Black-necked stilt at Salton Sea.
Bottom: Spinning wind turbines in the valley's western pass generate non-polluting energy.

Facing page: Snow-covered pines at the top of San Jacinto frame the sun-drenched floor of the Coachella Valley in mid-winter.

19

From snow-covered peaks

to desert burrows and

inland seas to palm-circled

springs, California's desert

resort area is a natural

wonder.

generated more than 450 million kilowatts, enough to service a community of 75,000 homes for a full year.

South and east of the desert resort area is still another natural wonder: Anza-Borrego Desert State Park. This 600,000-acre park is the largest in the California system. It covers almost one fifth of San Diego County and parts of Riverside and Imperial counties. Its split name is derived from Captain Juan Bautista de Anza, an early Spanish explorer, and the *borrego*, the yearling male ram that lives in the park.

Elevations in Anza-Borrego range from 500 to above 6,000 feet. Flash floods from the park's higher points have, over centuries, caused severe gullies and sharp ridges that give the area a moon-like appearance. The lower area is known as the Borrego Badlands, named by early stagecoach drivers.

Paths of early explorers and prospectors in the park now form a network of roads, some still unpaved, that crisscross many scenic points. Surrounded by, but not part of the park, is the mountain community of Borrego Springs, a growing tourist resort and rest area for travelers.

A sharp drop from Anza-Borrego to the east at the south end of the Salton Sea is Imperial County, now one of the richest farming lands in the world. This northern tip of the great Sonoran Desert is irrigated by a chain of canals from the Colorado River. Today, the region is a leading producer of lettuce, cattle feed, and a host of vegetables shipped year-round to the rest of the nation.

In contrast to the lush farmland spreading south to the Mexican border, the eastern edge of the Imperial Valley is home of the Algodones Sand Dunes. Reaching peaks of more than 300 feet, these dunes are, in approved areas, a popular area for off-road vehicles. The dune buggies leave many tracks after busy weekends but the winds blowing west out of Anza-Borrego soon restore them to their natural state. The constant wind relentlessly moves the dunes eastward, about one foot each year.

"The Coachella Valley is part of the largest area of dry land in the Western Hemisphere," said Beach Leighton, noted geologist and Professor Emeritus at Whittier College. "It is filled with youthful, 60-million-year-old sedimentary deposits as much as 20,000 feet deep. The active San Andreas fault system lends a little excitement to the valley," Leighton points out, "and the Mission Creek Fault just north and parallel to Interstate 10 provides access to the surface for heated underground water."

Born of earthquakes, oceans, winds and mistakes, California's desert resort area has had its beauty burnished by the frequent wind-blown sands. From snow-covered peaks to desert burrows and inland seas to palm-circled springs, it's a natural wonder.

GEORGE SERVICE

Left: Bighorn ram at Living Desert.

Facing page: Algodones sand dunes in protected area near Glamis late in afternoon.

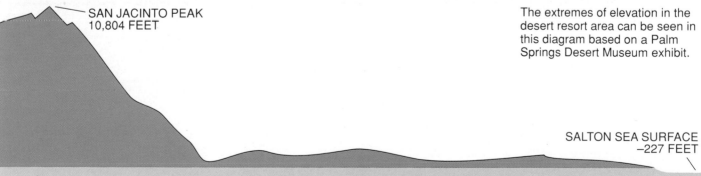

SAN JACINTO PEAK
10,804 FEET

The extremes of elevation in the desert resort area can be seen in this diagram based on a Palm Springs Desert Museum exhibit.

SALTON SEA SURFACE
−227 FEET

LINDA COLLINS

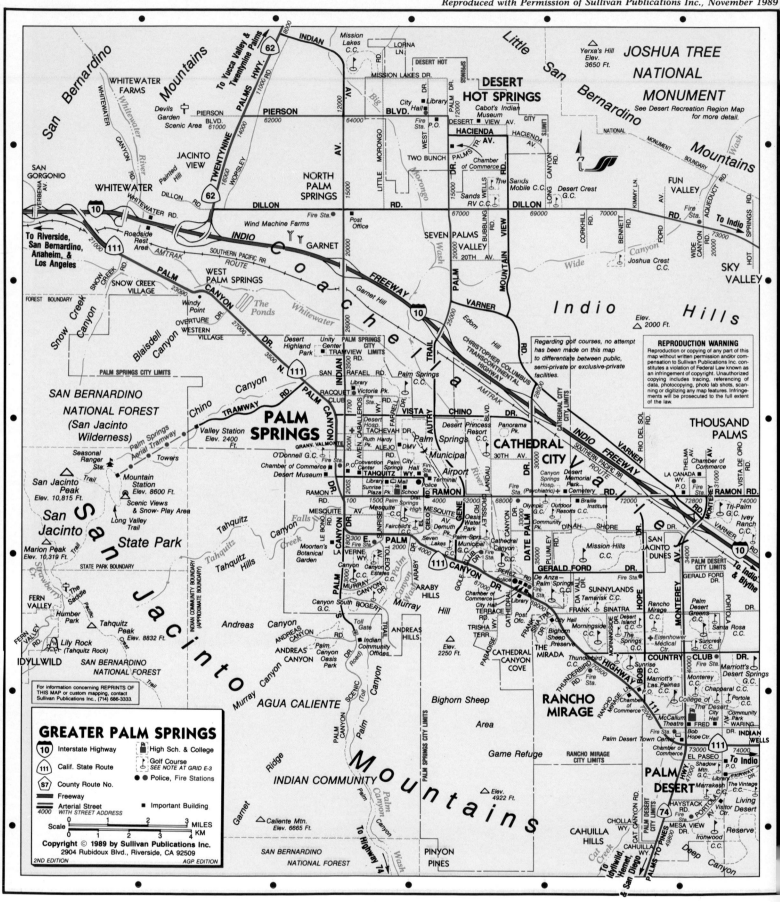

GREATER PALM SPRINGS

- **10** Interstate Highway
- **111** Calif. State Route
- **S7** County Route No.
- Freeway
- Arterial Street
- 4000 WITH STREET ADDRESS
- 🏫 High Sch. & College
- ⛳ Golf Course SEE NOTE AT GRID E-3
- ● Police, Fire Stations
- ■ Important Building

Scale
0 1 2 3 MILES
0 1 2 3 4 KM

Copyright © 1989 by Sullivan Publications Inc.
2904 Rubidoux Blvd., Riverside, CA 92509

2ND EDITION   AGP EDITION

For information concerning REPRINTS of THIS MAP or custom mapping, contact Sullivan Publications, Inc., (714) 686-3333.

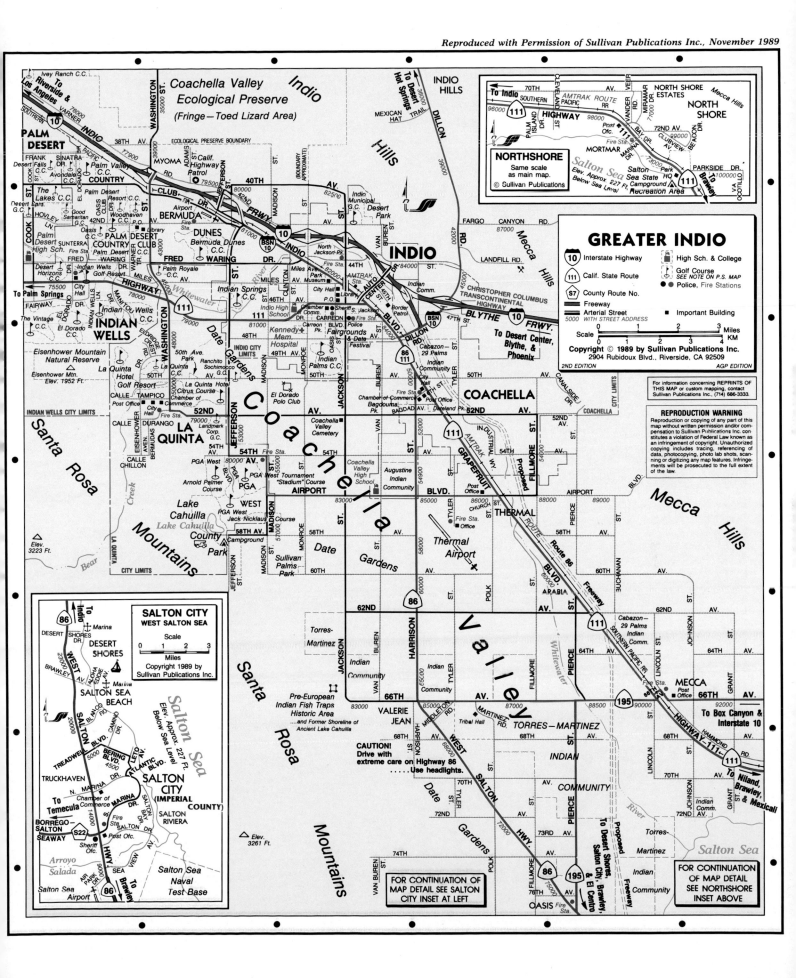

GREATER INDIO

- **10** Interstate Highway
- **111** Calif. State Route
- **S7** County Route No.
- Freeway
- Arterial Street — 5000 WITH STREET ADDRESS
- High Sch. & College
- Golf Course — SEE NOTE ON P.S. MAP
- ● ● Police, Fire Stations
- ■ Important Building

Scale — 0 1 2 3 Miles / 0 1 2 3 4 KM

Copyright © 1989 by Sullivan Publications Inc.
2904 Rubidoux Blvd., Riverside, CA 92509

2ND EDITION   AGP EDITION

For information concerning REPRINTS OF THIS MAP or custom mapping, contact Sullivan Publications Inc., (714) 686-3333.

REPRODUCTION WARNING
Reproduction or copying of any part of this map without written permission and/or compensation to Sullivan Publications Inc. constitutes a violation of Federal Law known as an infringement of copyright. Unauthorized copying includes tracing, referencing of data, photocopying, photo lab shots, scanning or digitizing any map features. Infringements will be prosecuted to the full extent of the law.

NORTHSHORE
Same scale as main map.
© Sullivan Publications

SALTON CITY
WEST SALTON SEA
Scale 0 1 2 3 Miles
Copyright 1989 by Sullivan Publications Inc.

CAUTION! Drive with extreme care on Highway 86 ..... Use headlights.

FOR CONTINUATION OF MAP DETAIL SEE SALTON CITY INSET AT LEFT

FOR CONTINUATION OF MAP DETAIL SEE NORTHSHORE INSET ABOVE

Coachella Valley Ecological Preserve (Fringe—Toed Lizard Area)

23

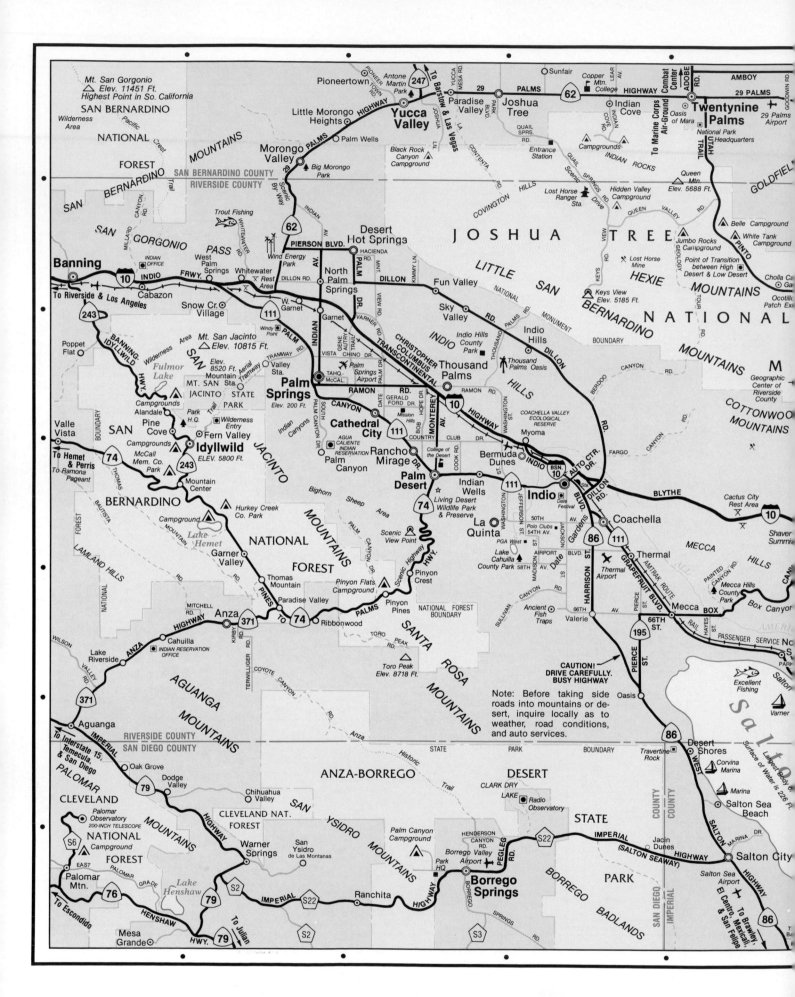

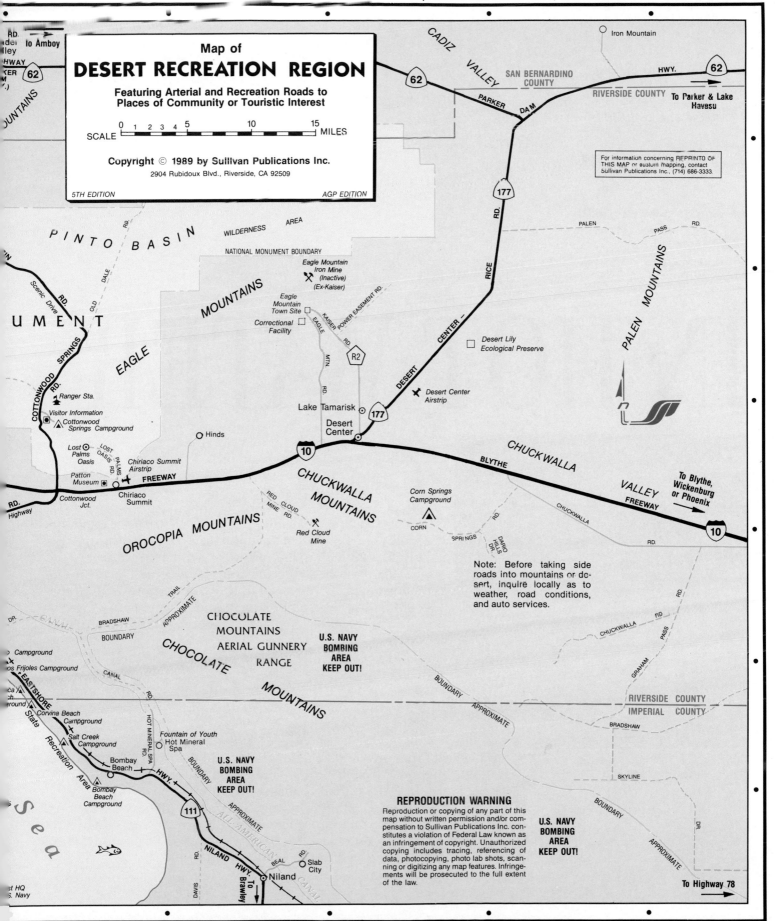

Reproduced with Permission of Sullivan Publications Inc., November 1989

Map of
DESERT RECREATION REGION

Featuring Arterial and Recreation Roads to Places of Community or Touristic Interest

SCALE 0 1 2 3 4 5 10 15 MILES

Copyright © 1989 by Sullivan Publications Inc.

2904 Rubidoux Blvd., Riverside, CA 92509

5TH EDITION   AGP EDITION

Iron Mountain

CADIZ VALLEY

SAN BERNARDINO COUNTY

62

62

HWY.

PARKER DAM

RIVERSIDE COUNTY   To Parker & Lake Havasu

177

PALEN   PASS   RD.

RICE   RD.

PINTO BASIN

WILDERNESS AREA

NATIONAL MONUMENT BOUNDARY

Scenic Drive   RD.

OLD DALE RD.

EAGLE   MOUNTAINS

PALEN MOUNTAINS

Eagle Mountain Iron Mine (Inactive) (Ex-Kaiser)

Eagle Mountain Town Site

Correctional Facility

KAISER POWER EASEMENT RD.

EAGLE MTN. RD.

R2

DESERT   CENTER

Desert Lily Ecological Preserve

MENT

UMENT

Cottonwood Springs RD.

Ranger Sta.

Visitor Information

Cottonwood Springs Campground

Hinds

Lake Tamarisk

Desert Center

177

Desert Center Airstrip

Lost Palms Oasis

LOST OASIS RD.

LOST PALMS RD.

Patton Museum

Chiriaco Summit Airstrip

FREEWAY

10

CHUCKWALLA

BLYTHE

Corn Springs Campground

CHUCKWALLA   VALLEY   FREEWAY

To Blythe, Wickenburg or Phoenix

RD. Highway

Cottonwood Jct.

Chiriaco Summit

CHUCKWALLA MOUNTAINS

CORN

SPRINGS

DARIO HILLS DR.

RD.

CHUCKWALLA

RD.

10

 OROCOPIA MOUNTAINS

RED CLOUD MINE RD.

Red Cloud Mine

RD.

CHUCKWALLA   PASS

GRAHAM

Note: Before taking side roads into mountains or desert, inquire locally as to weather, road conditions, and auto services.

TRAIL

APPROXIMATE

BRADSHAW

BOUNDARY

CHOCOLATE MOUNTAINS AERIAL GUNNERY RANGE

U.S. NAVY BOMBING AREA KEEP OUT!

CHOCOLATE   MOUNTAINS

RD.

CANAL

BOUNDARY

APPROXIMATE

RIVERSIDE COUNTY

IMPERIAL COUNTY

BRADSHAW

Campground

os Frijoles Campground

EASTSHORE

State Recreation Area

Corvina Beach Campground

Salt Creek Campground

HOT MINERAL SPA RD.

Fountain of Youth Hot Mineral Spa

Bombay Beach

Bombay Beach Campground

Sea

HWY.

ALL-AMERICAN

BOUNDARY   APPROXIMATE

U.S. NAVY BOMBING AREA KEEP OUT!

SKYLINE

BOUNDARY   APPROXIMATE

DR.

111

NILAND HWY.

RD.

BEAL RD.

DAVIS RD.

Slab City

Niland

To Brawley

CANAL

st HQ
S. Navy

U.S. NAVY BOMBING AREA KEEP OUT!

To Highway 78

25

CHAPTER TWO

When they came to the hot

springs bubbling among

the palms, the Cahuilla In-

dians' ancestors recognized

the water's curative quali-

ties and chose to stay.

IN HOT WATER

C ascadians, who probably crossed the Arctic ice-shelf on the Bering Sea more than 20,000 years ago, fanned out across the far west of what is now North America.

Their descendants arrived in the Coachella Valley on their bicontinental trek south to found the mighty Aztec, Mayan and Inca civilizations.

The scientists who dig into such things have found clues of "early horizon" culture, sometimes called the "Pinto Man" era, on the north plateau above the Coachella Valley. These artifacts date back more than 10,000 years.

Prehistoric camel bones and other fossils uncovered in the Indio and Mecca region indicate the area was once a verdant pastureland.

First evidence of the arrival of the early Cahuilla Indians indicates they camped and hunted in the Coachella Valley about 900 years ago.

S tep back in time now, 500 years or more, and pay a visit to the Agua Caliente Band of Mission Indians, a branch of the Cahuilla people. These were the original Palm Springs residents.

Like most other tribes in Southern California, these courageous people belong to the Shoshonean division of the Uto-Aztecan linguistic family. Tribes in this group range from the Mexican Aztecs to the Hopi, Papago and Pima of Arizona and the Colorado Ute.

Above: Gambrel quail chick learns how to strut. These beautiful birds abound in the desert resort area.

Facing page: Cahuilla Indian baskets were considered exceptional in design. Seen here is Dolores, wife of Francis Patencio, one of the last Agua Caliente ceremonial leaders, who was herself a noted basketmaker.

At "Gossip Rock" in An-

dreas Canyon, the Agua

Caliente women ground

meal while the men

worked leather and carved

arrowheads.

GEORGE SERVICE

As far as history records, Cahuilla ancestors realized the curative powers of the mineral springs in the palm oasis at the foot of the San Jacinto mountains. Bubbling to the surface at about 104 to 106 degrees, these waters carry with them therapeutic trace elements such as zinc, iron and magnesium, among many others.

In 1776, Juan de Anza and his trail-blazing expedition came upon the desert Indians enjoying the hot springs. He called them the Agua Caliente, Spanish for "hot water." A most appropriate name, for over the ensuing centuries, these intrepid Indians have been in hot water in more ways than one.

The early Agua Caliente lived in a virtual silence. One century-ago observer noted, "A strange and somber loneliness hangs over the village, especially at night fall." Their exuberance was saved, perhaps, for the ceremonial occasions, which were numerous. There were Cahuilla ceremonies for birth, death, puberty, marriage, hunting and more. When they did communicate, early writers speak of "Cahuilla-babel," apparently because each tribe, indeed each sub-group, seemed to have a separate language. It is thought that this complexity brought them to adopt many common Spanish words and phrases, despite their isolation from the missions.

Daily life of these Southern California natives was both very simple and fraught with problems. Starvation, of course, was a constant threat.

Before introduction of cultivated crops, the search for seasonal foods occupied all members of the tribe. While other pressures then were few, food gathering was necessary and constant. Staples consisted of cactus, palm nuts, mesquite pods and acorns, which were ground into meal. Many Agua Caliente mortars and pestles have been found over the years in the Indian Canyons.

In Andreas Canyon, one large rock, known as "Gossip Rock," is where women gathered to grind meal. This same area was a gathering spot for males, also, as a saw-tooth projection in the rock is thought to be where they drew leather to make it pliable. Scientists also have found evidence of arrowhead-making there.

Climatic changes forced different plants to bloom at different times of the year and brought variety to the Indians' diet. Wild cherry, plum and grapes might be gathered on one trip up the canyons and mountainsides, while another season brought forth cactus, yucca and agave. Like cabbage, agave could be roasted, boiled or dried. Barrel cactus was cooked in a pit between layers of coals covered with dampened sand. It was then cut up and used in stews. Yucca, said to taste like asparagus, was eaten either fresh or boiled.

Meat for the family was a male responsibility. With sticks and longbows, men hunted bear, jaguar, deer, sheep and rabbit. The meat was often dried and stored in ollas, or jars.

The people spent summers in the canyons where lofty palms, natural

Tahquitz Falls in Tahquitz Canyon.

caves and clear streams brought welcome relief from the arid desert sands. In winter, however, when mountain streams turned icy and caves' rock walls chilled, the Indians retreated again to the warmth of the valley floor and the many palm oases and heated waters.

"For raising children, there was nothing like it," noted Dr. John Harrington in the book *Southern California Indians.* "The kids could wallow in the mud all day, could play throwing it at each other, could climb trees without a rip, wrestle without losing a button and could play sliding down the great sleek rocks, as they often did, without fear of wearing out anything but their own behinds.

"There was no making or buying of clothes for the youngsters, no washing, no mending and as for spanking, one did not even have the trouble of letting their pants down. Furthermore, the custom was most demo-

"Fig Tree John" was named for the many fig trees he nurtured near his home at the Salton Sea. One of the best known of the Cahuillas, he was said to be 136 years old when he died in 1927.

cratic for the children of the poor or lazy looked as handsome as those of the rich. It reduced the work and worry of raising children to one fourth," Harrington concluded, "and the expense to merely that of food."

Each daybreak year-round, the family arose and headed for the nearest water to bathe. This was usually before the moon had set and the sun edged up the temperature.

More fortunate than many, the desert Cahuillas were spared much of the barbarities of the white explorer and settler periods because of their basic isolation in Se-Khi—their name for what is today Palm Springs.

Their dwellings, called Kish, usually large enough for an extended family, were circular brush shelters built over scooped-out hollows. Later years saw them erect rectangular homes with mud or adobe walls and thatched roofs, a Mexican *jacal* influence.

From each Cahuilla village of 100 to 200 people, trails formed a network to other villages and hunt-

PALM SPRINGS HISTORICAL SOCIETY

ing grounds. Several villages together composed a tribelet, a larger territorial unit.

By nature a gentle people, with a great sense of family, the Cahuilla Indians chose their leaders carefully. Even today, they speak of one of their own as having power, but their meaning is older and, perhaps, more important than today's meaning. They did not mean great physical, political or financial strength, but a spiritual or mental strength, a strength of character. Each person with this power was, and is, by the Indian, called "Master."

Other Mission Indians in the area didn't fare nearly as well as the Agua Caliente, because under Spanish—and later under Mexican—rule, they were terribly exploited. Draconian policies and conditions close to slavery existed for many tribes living near white settlements.

Until completion of the railroad, settlers and visitors arrived in Palm Springs via horse-drawn conveyances on the Bradshaw Trail, an early stage route from Los Angeles to Yuma, Arizona.

After a Spanish captain wrote in 1823 of an Indian group he "discovered" living by a hot spring in the desert, life for the Agua Caliente was to never again be the same.

In the 1850s, government topographers sought a way west for railroads to link the Mississippi River and the Pacific Ocean. Their explorations followed basically the route of their Spanish predecessors, except they found the San Gorgonio Pass. Earlier routes had followed a treacherous path across the mountains.

A young Army Lieutenant, R.S. Williamson, reported finding in the desert a friendly, healthy people who had adapted themselves to their unique environment and enjoyed a climatic oasis around the hot springs.

Trusting Indians not only helped in building irrigation projects, in farming and maintaining stagecoach stops, they even helped build the

The "iron horse" and the

white settlers who came

with it brought harmful

changes to the Mission

tribes, from illness to ex-

tremely repressive laws.

railroad. The "iron horse" brought more, however, than technology. A violent bout of smallpox soon wiped out many Indians. Measles, changes in diet and general harassment by white settlers killed off many from the Mission tribes.

Harry James, in his book *The Cahuilla Indians*, showed the Indian population cut 70 percent under Spanish rule, with 30 percent of the survivors perishing under Mexican rule. And, perhaps more shameful, between 1848 and 1880, the rest of the California Indians were diminished by more than 80 percent under American rule.

It wasn't just "frontier law" and the gun-holster philosophy of "the only good Indian is a dead Indian" that destroyed these people. The early frontier system had no place in it for the Indian. If they were docile and "fit

GEORGE SERVICE PHOTOS

in" peacefully, they were allowed. If they didn't, they were exterminated or segregated onto reservations, almost equally bad consequences in the eyes of the freedom-loving natives.

Nor did the government help. In fact, in the mid-1800s, the California legislature passed three laws the Indians never shall forget: The first denied any Indian the right to testify in court; the second said the word of any white man could have any Indian declared a vagrant and sold at auction; and the third, according to the James study, allowed any Indian to be bound over to a white person for years of labor and paid only in subsistence.

Under earlier Spanish rule, Mission Indians who deserted were whipped with rawhide. If they persisted, they were branded or disfigured, James reported. Under what might have been the gentle hand of religion, the character of these simple people was all but destroyed.

Left to right: Snow plant near Idyllwild.
Sand verbena in Palm Springs.
Robusta palm frond in Palm Springs.
Barrel cactus blossom in Palm Canyon.

Those fortunate enough came to live with the desert Cahuillas, who were still too remote to come under the direct influence of the explorers. Accordingly, the Agua Caliente had been able to retain much of their early culture.

Francisco Patencio, born in the mid-1800s, and later Chief of the Agua Caliente Tribe, put it perhaps too gently when he said, "The way of the Indians was very hard. First, he learned the way of the Spanish...then the way of the Mexican. Then, he had to learn again...the way of the white man. The Indian could not please everyone."

"They had been tricked and defrauded so many times," James wrote, "that they are suspicious of every proposition that is presented. They are rugged individualists, which makes tribal policy difficult."

In its urgency to complete a transcontinental rail passage, the U.S.

Indian-style blankets—using the colors of desert plants as seen on the facing page—and jewelry often are seen at "swap" meets and special event sales in desert cities.

government awarded land along the desert route to the railroads. It gave odd-numbered sections (each a mile square) to the rail builders, while even-numbered sections became reservation lands. From that day on, the desert real estate maps have resembled a giant checker-board. This checker-boarding would turn out to be both good news and bad news for the area Indians.

Finally, in 1877, the Southern Pacific chugged its first train from Yuma, Arizona through the desert and pass into a nascent Los Angeles.

The Agua Caliente, like Indians of other areas in the United States, considered their ancestral lands to be their own property. It was, needless to say, difficult for them to accept the "purchase" of railroad land by others.

Little realized then, but hidden in this takeover more than a century ago, were the beginnings of a chain of events that would make this tribe one of the wealthiest in the nation.

For many years, the government paid scant attention to the concerns of the Mission Indians. Their situation went from bad to worse until, in 1884, Helen Hunt Jackson published her novel *Ramona*. This now-classic tale told of whites' killing of Indians in such detail that it aroused a public outcry for long-delayed justice for the true native Californians.

Seven years later, Congress passed the Mission Indian Relief Act authorizing allotments for each band of Mission Indians. In 1886, the first trust patent was issued to the Agua Caliente. Subsequent trust patents in the early 1900s saw land totalling 31,127 acres allotted to the tribe (including Section 14, which today is downtown Palm Springs). However, more than 50 years would pass before these allotments were approved by the Department of the Interior. And, only a little more than a decade ago, did the Indians receive rights to control zoning on their land. Each of the tribal members was entitled to receive 47 acres of land: two in the city, five of irrigated land, and 40 acres of desert on grazing land. Today, the Agua Caliente are allowed to lease their land for up to 99 years.

Richard Milanovich, current chairman of the Agua Caliente Tribal Council, says there are currently about 265 members of the tribe, about one quarter of whom are full-blooded Indians. Besides the fees collected from visitors to their canyons, the tribe realizes substantial income from the lease of land and the original spa to Palm Springs merchants and valley developers. Milanovich explains that since the zoning determination in the late 1970s, they have signed agreements with Palm Springs and Cathedral City to enable a mutual approach to resolving zoning matters. A similar arrangement is planned with Riverside County concerning the unincorporated areas of the valley.

Seldom are tribal ceremonies conducted anymore. "We are attempting to hold onto the culture," 46-year-old Milanovich laments, "but it is becoming more and more difficult as time passes." The Tribal Council does plan an Indian Interpretive Center in Tahquitz Canyon. As might be expected, this center has been some time in coming and is currently working its way through the quagmire of the white man's bureaucracy.

Characterizing their traditional way of life, James reported of the Cahuilla people that "with all our dentistry, the Indians suffered not one tenth the pain with their teeth we do. With all our agriculture and stock raising, the Indians ate more wholesome food than we do...It is sometimes refreshing for a moment to forget our rigid standpoint of superiority and to dream our way back to simple customs, which under-population made possible, and to praise them.

MARK THOMPSON

"The courage, integrity, intelligence, imagination, tenacity, pungent sense of humor, and dramatic flair [of the Cahuillas]...are evident in their descendants who are among us today. They moved from a primitive culture a century ago," James concluded, "into today's complex culture with amazing grace. Not all easy steps but in a century they have spanned eons."

Without question, the Agua Caliente Indians now are financially secure. Belatedly, the wrongs have been righted. Today they are admired and envied by their Indian brothers and sisters across the country, and respected by their "new" neighbors in Se-Khi.

Above: *Undeveloped Indian-owned land in the middle of Palm Springs.*

Facing page: *An Indian jeweler and his wares at a valley sale.*

"...an uninhabited country..."

that Indians feared...

IN ONE ERA... AND OUT THE OTHER

Hernando de Alarcon's galleon sailed northward up the Gulf of California and the Colorado River to about what is today Needles, California. The year was 1540. It's thought he and his expedition were probably the first non-Indians to visit what is today Riverside County.

A century and a half passed before the missionaries began their many tours into the then-desolate region. Father Eusebio Francisco Kino crossed the Colorado River in 1701 into the lower Colorado Desert. Seventy-some years later, Captain Juan Bautista de Anza explored the Borrego Valley and San Jacinto Mountains, opening a route from Mexico to San Francisco. In 1849, gold fever in California attracted prospectors to the area. The following year, California became a state. But of the desert area, even a decade later, an army captain wrote:

"I consider it an immense waste of uninhabited country, incapable of cultivation without irrigation...even the Indians think of this desert with terror. They believe the souls of bad Indians are condemned to wander over the desert forever, in summer without water, and in winter without clothing."

Pedro Chino's small ranch was a simple one-room adobe structure between the hot spring and the San Jacinto Mountains. He had planted a few fruit trees and irrigated them as well as he could.

One day, in 1880, a most unusual meeting occurred. From out of the west arrived two white men who offered the Indian $150 for his property. He readily accepted and the first Palm Springs real estate deal was sealed. Over the next few years the two men expanded their land holdings but lived elsewhere, not unlike many modern-day investors.

Into this scene, in 1884, came a tall, troubled man seeking a healthful spot for his young son, John. "Judge" John Guthrie McCallum, a San Francisco attorney, first moved his family to San Bernardino in his search for a drier climate. Young John suffered with tuberculosis.

Years before, the elder McCallum had traveled east to cast California's

San Jacinto Mountain at sunrise takes on hues from red to purple and chocolate brown, depending on the blowing sand and the time of year.

Judge McCallum's 19-mile, stone-lined ditch bringing water to his fledgling orchards was the Colorado desert's first irrigation project.

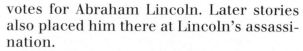

votes for Abraham Lincoln. Later stories also placed him there at Lincoln's assassination.

In San Bernardino, the Judge represented the government in Indian affairs. It was in this way he met Will Pablo, an Indian scout and interpreter, who told him of the beautiful water and air in a desert area known as Agua Caliente. Once having seen it, he again decided to move.

On March 24, 1885, several months after the McCallum family was settled in this new location, the Judge purchased an interest from the two investors in a part of the original 320-acre transaction. A most meaningful day for the family became an historic day for the area... Judge McCallum had just become the first white settler to make Palm Springs his permanent home.

To house his family—wife Emily, sons John, Wallace and Harry, and daughters May and Pearl—McCallum had the local Indians help him build an adobe home. He went about planting orchards, buying adjacent land and telling all he could contact about what he called his "Palm Valley." In time, he owned some 6,000 acres. And he had a grand dream.

In the desert, water is always problem number one. For the McCallums, a source of clear water was a pressing need. Because of the region's early growing season, he felt he could beat other California growers to the Los Angeles market. But for his fledgling orchards to grow, he needed water.

Drawing on unskilled labor and using what tools existed, McCallum financed a 19-mile, stone-lined ditch from Whitewater to his land. This was the first irrigation project in the Colorado desert.

At McCallum's incessant urging, prospective land purchasers were attracted. But in the middle of the desert, what was he to do with them? The resourceful Judge enticed an eccentric Scotsman from Banning, named Welwood Murray, to move out into the desert. On land leased from McCallum, and across from the family adobe, Murray built the small Palm Springs Hotel, which opened in 1886.

Judge John G. McCallum was the first white settler to make Palm Springs his family home.

No slouch at promoting his interests, the now "Dr." Murray hired a local Indian to greet the trains that stopped near Whitewater. Astride a camel, resplendent in an Arab costume, Murray's barker passed out pamphlets on Palm Valley and the Palm Springs Hotel.

Murray soon leased the soul of the community, the hot springs, from the Indians and built a bath house for his hotel guests. The desert resort era had begun—sort of.

McCallum's dream expanded when three new promoters began development of Palmdale, a site not far from his own and today called Smoke Tree Ranch. Arabs on camels may have suited Murray, but this new trio gave tourism a swift kick into the future by building their own narrow-gauge rail spur. Connecting with the Southern Pacific line 12 miles northwest of their property, the little wood-burning locomotive

Itinerant cowboys in the late 1890s found water at the old Indian Well, which replaced the early hand-dug Indian well that gave the community its name.

and two used San Francisco streetcars were to carry prospective buyers in style.

But it turned into "the little train that couldn't." After a brief time, Palmdale failed. The train was left to rot in the desert heat. All that was useable were the rail ties, which later played their own role in history.

Palmdale died but the Judge's dream endured. He sold land to farmers who expanded plantings in the valley to include alfalfa, grapes, corn and citrus.

"The only spot in California where frost, fog and windstorms are absolutely unknown," read the poster promoting a special land auction train from San Francisco to McCallum's Palm Valley in October 1887. After the train arrived at the station, the passengers traveled by carriage to Murray's hotel, where they prepared for the following day's land auction. And quite an auction it turned out to be. The first lot sold for $50; the next two for $45 each. In all, 136 parcels were sold that day. Their descendants today may well rue the fact that nearly all those buyers later let the state take their properties for non-payment of taxes.

And then the unthinkable happened—twice! In 1893, it began to rain. And rain it did, continuously, for almost three weeks. The hard-built water ditches disappeared in the deluge. And then nature (perhaps the demon Tahquitz?) struck again with a 10-year drought that killed the cattle and crops.

McCallum's farmers left as fast as they had arrived a decade earlier. His sons had died of illnesses. His dream had become a nightmare. In debt and despair, he died in 1897, leaving 6,000 acres, some water shares and equipment to his wife and remaining children.

Emily McCallum died in 1914, and the family's remaining heir was young Pearl, who was yet to play a pivotal role in the development of her father's land.

Welwood Murray stayed on, somehow. And in 1905, just as the Colorado River burst its banks to form the Salton Sea, the rains returned. For those who had remained, it was the beginning of a new era of growth.

Above: Derelict cable cars, part of the ill-fated Palmdale railroad spur, were left to rot in the desert sun when the project failed in 1887.

Facing page: Early morning sun lights the canyon walls forming the shadow called "The Tahquitz Witch." In this early photograph, palm trees were being hauled to the King Gillette estate.

* * *

"Mother" Coffman's hotel, The Desert Inn, almost never happened. Mrs. Nellie Coffman, daughter of a Santa Monica hotel man, had once passed the Palm Springs area on a train trip. She remembered the peace and solitude of the tiny town. Near Christmas, in 1908, she returned with her son Earl, and stayed at the only place in town, Dr. Murray's Palm Springs Hotel. Her interest in the desert went from spark to flame.

One year later she returned with her husband, Dr. Harry Coffman, and both of her sons, George Robertson (by her first marriage) and Earl. The Coffmans bought a small existing sanatorium. (Many who came to the desert at that time, like McCallum's son John in the 1800s, made the journey to alleviate tuberculosis.)

With water again available and crops returning, visitors also returned

41

to the desert. As business grew, Mrs. Coffman added tent houses to her complex, and then purchased the adjoining property. Thus was born what was to become the internationally acclaimed Desert Inn. With her sons' considerable help, hotel business flourished.

About this time, a trio of women arrived who also would leave a major mark. Dr. Florilla White from New York, and her sisters Cornelia and Isabel, purchased the Palm Springs Hotel. Founder Dr. Murray had died in 1914.

The White sisters proceeded to buy the rest of the block south of their hotel, the current location of The Plaza. Miss Cornelia managed to have a wooden home built. The wood had been reclaimed from the nearby desert, the ties from the ill-fated Palmdale rail spur. (Today, Miss Cornelia's rail-tie home, as well as Judge McCallum's original adobe, are the centerpieces of the Village Green Heritage Center on South Palm Canyon Drive. She donated both the historic structure and the site for the first Desert Museum.)

Every Old West village had its characters. For Palm Springs it was Peter Pester, a hermit who lived in the Indian Canyons. Pester sold arrowheads, handmade canes and postcards. As former Palm Springs mayor Frank Bogert said, "Pester was a 'nature boy,' putting on clothes...when curious canyon visitors came into view." Pester had acquired a telescope and on weekends in town charged 10 cents to look at Lincoln's reclining profile on the west canyon wall.

Returning to Palm Springs in the early 1920s, Pearl McCallum, then Mrs. McManus, was a virtual outsider. Coffman's Desert Inn was bustling and across the way the White sisters managed growth at the Palm Springs Hotel. What to do? Pearl and her husband, Austin, found financing, hired an architect named Lloyd Wright and built—what else?—a hotel.

Within the year, across the street, "Mother" Coffman tore down the tent houses and made the first major addition to The Desert Inn.

In his book *Palm Springs—The First Hundred Years*, Bogert, the "Cowboy Mayor," related: "Life in the village was slow and easy...It consisted of checking at The Desert Inn for any new and interesting guests, stopping at Carl Lykken's store and post office for the

Above: Founder of The Desert Inn, Nellie Coffman was instrumental in creating the desert resort concept.

Facing page: Originally a sanitorium, The Desert Inn grew to become an internationally known resort in the heart of Palm Springs. The $100-million Desert Fashion Plaza is on this site today.

mail…walking down the street to say hello…or listening to the gossip at Dr. Kocher's drug store." Bogert, then 17, had arrived in Palm Springs with a string of horses he had inherited. He found a place to stable the horses on the Indian reservation and settled in.

By then Palm Springs had its first library, a low wooden building at the rear of the Community Church. At first it operated on the honor system, but as the collection grew, a custodian and later a full-time librarian watched over it. A school had also been erected and Ted McKinney, the first

PALM SPRINGS HISTORICAL SOCIETY PHOTOS BOTH PAGES

white child born in Palm Springs, remembers it well. "We would run off barefoot to the school in the morning, already waiting for school to end. When it did, we'd scurry up Tahquitz Canyon, catch a wild pony and ride until supper time." Today a robust 70-year-old, McKinney recalls those days with a twinkle in his eyes. "Perhaps," McKinney said, "the children in the family were invited to the first local school because they 'needed six and a fraction' kids each day to receive county and state aid. There were about 10 Indian families and 10 white families here then." (McKinney became a pilot in World War II, flying the "hump" from Burma to India and China before again settling back in Palm Springs. He is now chairman of the Indian Planning Commission, an advisory group established to assist the Tribal Council. He also served on the City Council for 12 years.)

The pace of progress picked up and, in the late 1920s, Palm Springs saw its first telephone installed at the local store, with an extension at The Desert Inn. A natural gas line connected the growing community with Banning in 1929. Electricity lines had arrived about six years before. Many tourists who no longer could travel to Europe during World War I had found the desert resort area. In the 1920s, as many as 35,000 annual visitors were counted in the Indian Canyons, publicized by an effort to name them a national monument.

43

From The Desert Inn, Nellie Coffman sent a stream of correspondence to the nation's news media extolling the quality of desert life and, of course, her hotel. Originally, her Desert Inn could accommodate only 13 guests and her slogan was "not the biggest, but the best." In time, the inn grew in reputation and size and easily could host more than 200 travellers. Nellie pointed a prescient finger at the future when she grabbed onto a railroad man's comment and described her holdings as "America's Foremost Desert Resort."

Nellie sold some of her mountainside holdings to an oilman, Tom O'Donnell. On it he built a mansion called "Ojo del Desierto"—the Eye of the Desert. More importantly, perhaps, he built his own nine-hole golf course adjoining the inn. A precedent had been established for the "Golf Capital of the World."

By the late 1920s, famous people from throughout the world were spending winters in luxurious, Spanish-styled guest houses amid an immaculate garden oasis. And, in the middle of this 35-acre paradise, they could cool themselves in the first Palm Springs swimming pool.

With the start of the 1930s, it was the end of the beginning for Palm Springs.

PALM SPRINGS HISTORICAL SOCIETY

Above: *Rudolph Valentino was one of the many early movie celebrities who made frequent desert visits. Here he is entertained by Peter Pester, known as the Hermit of Palm Springs.*

Facing page: *Even young golfers take lessons seriously at the Golf Institute of the Desert in Palm Desert.*

TED McKINNEY

Six-year-old Ted McKinney had to pull on his hand-me-down jeans before sunup. With his seven brothers and sisters, he would eat a quick breakfast of egg-battered, fried bread and head down Main Street to school. His older brothers already would have fed the chickens and milked the family cow.

It was 1925; the school was new. "They got it ready just for me," Ted said.

It sure was different living in town instead of in the old concrete house his father built on a homesteading ranch in the Morongo Valley. Up there it was green and cool, and the squash grew fat and the corn grew tall. In "town" it was just plain hot. But Ted's father dug wells and the few local residents needed water badly.

His mother knew the heat. Twice a day—120 degrees outside or not—she fired up the woodstove to cook the family meals. With no electricity, gas or running water, keeping and cooking food was no easy task. (Water dripped from a five-gallon drum onto a burlap sack on top of the cooling box. It would evaporate, keeping milk and foods cooler than without it—but not much.)

Miss Katherine Finchy, the school principal, would be waiting for the children about 8 a.m. But, more often than not, Harry Reed would have talked them into a quick softball game in front of his clinic. Of course, he always got to bat first.

At lunchtime, Ted and the others would soon finish their usual cheese sandwiches and then go looking for Indian ponies to ride. "They weren't too big for us and were kind of docile," he recalls. "We got their attention with a little food and we could ride all day."

There was never any skipping school in those days. "Hell," Ted says, "there wasn't anything else to do if you did skip." After school, they would find a pony and "ride to Tahquitz Falls or go to the swimmin' hole at Greentree or Scorpion."

If not riding, they spent the afternoon in front of Lykken's General Store playing jacks or hopscotch. All the local children, white, Indian and black, played together. "There never was a language problem," Ted says, "we just played. We all knew a little Spanish, I guess—but probably just the dirty words."

But if afternoon chores weren't done on time, "Mother would send us across the way to pick a creosote twig to switch us with. If the one we brought back wasn't big enough, we had to keep going back until it was. And, if it was something real bad, we got paddled over our father's knee when he got home."

When it came time for high school, Ted and the others had to trek to Banning each day. "If you had library work or sports, like I did," Ted says,

Above: Ted McKinney said "Eli," his 13-year-old whippet, learned to kneel so it could pray for him.

Facing page: Palm Canyon Drive of Ted McKinney's youth bears little resemblance to the palm-lined shopping attraction of today.

46

"you would miss the bus and have to hitch-hike home. But, it was no problem. No drugs or heavy drinking on the road then. And everybody knew everybody else."

When school was out for the summer, Ted's older brothers would load up the family's old slant-nosed Franklin automobile and take him fishing on the Rogue River in Oregon. Camping out, they would have all their necessities in the two covered trunks their father had built onto the

PALM SPRINGS HISTORICAL SOCIETY

running-boards. On the way home, the old two-track dirt road up into Morongo Valley took a lot of driving skill, he remembers. "You had to know how to drive in sand. It was tricky. You had to learn to go slow or you would get stuck in the sand and have to be pulled out."

Day ended early at the McKinney home. In the shadow of Mt. San Jacinto, it was dark by dinner time. As the desert began its nightly cooling, the evening chores were completed. With the kerosene lantern trimmed low, Palm Spring's first-born white child and his family would settle in.

Today, Ted McKinney looks down bustling Palm Canyon Drive—the Main Street of his youth. He points to the old grammar school site: "They turned it into a senior citizen's center now." He laughs and quips, "I guess they're getting it ready for me a second time."

CHAPTER FOUR

When Americans flocked to

movies during the Great

STAR-STRUCK

Depression, busy stars re-

laxed at Palm Springs.

During the Great Depression, following the stock market crash of 1929, the American people escaped to neighborhood movie theaters. Hollywood was in high gear. And the people who made the movies…writers, actors and directors…escaped too, to Palm Springs.

The little desert resort became a mecca for the screen stars of the era, as well as royalty and business magnates. There was no lack of interesting things to do: sunrise horseback rides, tennis and lawn-bowling, starlets at poolside, Cathedral City gambling clubs, the nation's leading entertainers, plus fine wine and the best of food. And work wasn't far away. On desert locations, mimicking everything from Egypt to the South Pacific, more than 10 films a year were being made in the resort area.

Palm Springs' heyday had arrived.

For busy Hollywood stars in the early '30s, few things were as frustrating as not being able to get time on the tennis court when they wanted it.

Silent-film actor Charles Farrell and his film-friend Ralph Bellamy felt the nasty itch of jealousy strike when they were bounced off the only court at the two-year-old El Mirador Hotel. It seemed hotel guest Marlene Dietrich wanted to play. And she wanted to play then.

From such events does progress come.

Prescott T. Stevens, a Colorado cattleman, organized a company to build the El

48

Left: Polo has been popular in the desert resorts for decades.
Right: The Desert Riders, formed in 1930 to enjoy catered breakfasts on Tuesday morning rides, continues today, raising funds and maintaining 100 miles of equestrian trails in the valley.

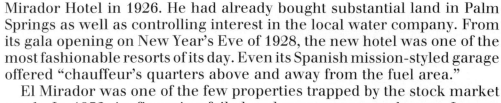

When the Racquet Club

opened in 1932, it cost only

$1 to play tennis there—but

the amenities included little

more than a wind-break.

Mirador Hotel in 1926. He had already bought substantial land in Palm Springs as well as controlling interest in the local water company. From its gala opening on New Year's Eve of 1928, the new hotel was one of the most fashionable resorts of its day. Even its Spanish mission-styled garage offered "chauffeur's quarters above and away from the fuel area."

El Mirador was one of the few properties trapped by the stock market crash. In 1932, its financing failed and new owners took over. It soon reopened, however, more splendid than before.

Hollywood found a winter home at the new El Mirador with its 75-foot swimming pool and impeccable amenities. It was one of the few facilities in Palm Springs that didn't have to change its stationery when the local fathers changed all the street names to the Indian names they have today. They were already on Indian Avenue, the only street to retain its original name.

Stage, screen and radio stars arrived with their staff to spend winters at El Mirador. For six winters, "Amos and Andy," a leading radio show of the 1930s, was broadcast daily by NBC from the El Mirador Tower. Freeman Gosden and Charlie Correll, Andy and Amos respectively, would write their material poolside by day and then perform over the air waves each evening at 7 p.m.

El Mirador's guest book included signatures that any autograph hound would die for: Cary Grant, Artie Shaw, Jack Benny, Gloria Swanson, Marilyn Monroe, Clark Gable, Albert Einstein, Ava Gardner—and even Howard Hughes, but he used a fictitious name.

But back to tennis-playing Charlie and Ralph. In a fit of pique, worthy of a John McEnroe, they stormed away vowing to build their own tennis court. And build they did! "We built two courts for $7,000. Everyone thought we were nuts," Farrell related years later to *The Desert Sun.* "Tennis courts generally cost half that much to install then. But we wanted good ones. We had to put up a substantial windscreen, so a serve wouldn't wind up in Indio."

On 200 acres of property in the windy area north of El Mirador, the two tennis buffs launched a legend in 1932 when the Racquet Club heard "love" for the first time. The club had no visitor accommodations when it began. And Farrell and Bellamy charged friends just $1 to play. They put in a wind-break of tamarisk trees and, later, dressing rooms, a cooler and the to-become-famous Bamboo Bar. A swimming pool and cottages were added as the crowd increased.

Farrell later purchased Bellamy's share of the club. He and his wife, Virginia Valli, ran it for the Hollywood elite for the decades that followed. A place to hide away and play tennis.

Cathedral City's 139 Club, one of several gambling clubs that sprang up in the valley in the 1930s and '40s, had an armed lookout tower. The clubs were shut down in a massive sheriff's raid in the late 1940s and, by the time this picture was made, the old 139 Club housed a Humane Society thrift shop.

But tennis and tanning weren't the only interests catered to. A quarry contractor, Travis Rogers, an aficionado of western wear and horses, opened The Ranch Club, which received the nickname of "The Mink and Manure Club." This quickly became a center for movie types and locals to mingle at barbecues and dances. Over the years, the club has had several faces, once as a western restaurant, then a night spot and finally a comedy club. Today, it is being converted into an office complex.

For the village of Palm Springs, the 1930s were busy times: The first Catholic church was finished; The Plaza, one of the first shopping centers in California, opened; the Indianoya, a tribal shop, began displaying weaving, baskets and pottery; plans for an airport were studied; and land

51

Above left: Bandleader and singer Rudy Vallee is flanked by Ralph Bellamy, left, and Charlie Farrell at the Racquet Club in 1939. The cake was a gift from the owner of a local gambling casino.
Right: Dorothy Lamour and Bill Howard, her husband, enjoying the Palm Springs Tennis Club in the 1940s.

was donated for the Welwood Murray Memorial Library. Highlight of the decade was incorporation as a city and appointment of the first City Council in 1938. Permanent residents then tallied 5,336.

But if the 1930s were a boomer, the 1940s began as a bummer.

Trials at the annual Desert Inn dog show heard the announcer break in with the grim news that early that morning, December 7, 1941, Pearl Harbor had been bombed by the Japanese. Like most of the nation, the audience reacted with stunned confusion.

With the declaration of war, the face of Palm Springs changed. There were still visitors, to be sure, but now many of them sported Army khaki instead of tennis white. And many were wounded.

Left: *El Mirador's tennis court drew the greats of Hollywood. Here, in 1932, Claudette Colbert serves a high one.*
Above: *World War II saw El Mirador turned into Torney General Hospital. The hotel-hospital's famous tower remained until destroyed by fire in 1989.*

During the war, the U.S. Army turned the El Mirador Hotel into Torney General Hospital. It expanded beyond the hotel's 30 acres to encompass more than 100 acres of barracks and medical facilities. The hospital staff of 1,300 treated 19,000 soldiers before the end of hostilities.

The U.S. Army engineers constructed a huge (by that day's standards) airfield on Indian land east of the city. Additional property was leased from Pearl McManus to build a service and personnel complex. A Ferry Command Center was established from which new aircraft were prepared and flown to the Pacific war zone.

Near mid-1942, General George S. Patton arrived in the desert with orders to establish a training command for the Army's tank operations. Those that knew "Old Blood and Guts" claim that when he first viewed his new hot and barren campground, he said, "This land isn't fit for life, but it's perfect for training soldiers."

Greg Carroll, curator of the General George S. Patton Museum in Chiriaco Summit, California, recently told *The Desert Sun* that about one quarter of all tank combat divisions that fought in World War II were trained at the desert center. The 18,000-square-mile training ground covered enormous areas of California, Arizona and Nevada.

PALM SPRINGS HISTORICAL SOCIETY PHOTOS BOTH PAGES

Carroll, a military historian, said not only were the new recruits unaccustomed to desert conditions, but they lacked necessary military equipment. One training center veteran recalled, "We were short of everything. We were lucky to have a tank. We used trucks with a big banner on them that said 'TANK'."

Those in training and those treated may not have enjoyed the experience but they remembered Palm Springs favorably. They and their families told their friends about the unique little palm-patch in the California desert. As Frank Bogert has said, "Palm Springs began hoppin' and jumpin'."

With the end of the war, development again picked up. The new Thunderbird Ranch opened, a few hundred homes were constructed, new schools completed—in all, more than $500,000 in building permits were issued the year after the war.

From the mid-1920s into the 1950s, American Indian jewelry, weavings and other items were sold at Indianoya, begun by trader Fred Watson.

Land between Palm Springs and Indio, about 30 miles to the east, had patiently waited its turn. Its time was now. From adjacent Cathedral City to Rancho Mirage and what would become Palm Desert, the lid came off. New homes, fire stations, subdivisions and country clubs took form. Still referred to by the old-timers in Palm Springs as "down-valley," these new communities got ready for their era of prosperity.

With the advent of the 1950s, the desert resort area was in full swing. The Riviera Hotel of Palm Springs (now the Radisson), with the area's first convention facility, was ready in 1952. The same year the refurbished El Mirador, back in private hands once more, reopened.

The original "hot springs" spa had, over a century, seen two makeshift

54

Left: Bob Hope, Frank Sinatra and Dean Martin gathered in Palm Springs for the 1963 Bob Hope Desert Golf Classic.
Right top: Dinah Shore, a valley resident for a quarter century, founded the annual Nabisco Dinah Shore LPGA Tournament held each spring near her home at Mission Hills Country Club in Rancho Mirage.
Bottom: Actor Robert Stack and his wife, Rosemary Bowe, on the courts at the Palm Springs Tennis Club in the 1950s.

bath houses erected over it. But the Agua Caliente Tribal Council was always reluctant to allow further development. In the late 1950s, a 99-year lease was finally signed and the world-class, five-story Spa Hotel at the intersection of Indian Avenue and Tahquitz was built. The tribe had an asset that would, along with their canyons, provide a long-term return.

Near the close of the decade, the visit of President Dwight D. Eisenhower touched off another publicity boom for Palm Springs. But of greater import to the local Indians, on his return to Washington he signed the long-awaited Equalization Bill, the final step in authorizing the Agua Caliente's equal land allotments.

"Condo-mania" was the term applied to the mushroom-like growth of second-home units in Southern California in the 1960s. Condominium law had to be written on state and local levels. It took time and effort but it worked. According to Bogert's history of the city, there are now more than 12,000 condos in Palm Springs alone, and the concept spilled over into the contiguous communities.

Palm Springs has been star-struck but never star-crossed. John Guthrie McCallum's dream has been more than fulfilled. From a humble adobe and a hand-dug ditch, a wonderland was born. Now "Golf Capital of the World," the California desert resort area is getting ready for its second hundred years.

We'll bet it breaks par!

COURTESY OF YVONNE CROSSLEY LOGGINS

Lawrence Crossley, one of the first black residents of Palm Springs, was an early investor in El Mirador Hotel. A prospector, politician and developer, Crossley managed the local water company, a restaurant and hotel. Crossley Road is near the Tramview mobile park, which he built 20 years before the tramway existed.

"EL GRANDOTE"

It was a weekend morning in late summer of '27 and the trail through the pass was dusty and hot. The tall, dark stranger, hat tilted down against the rising sun, rode slowly into the valley. He wore black. And behind him were a string of saddle horses. Riding with him was his partner Rod Abbott. The cowboy was a young man, perhaps no more than 17, but he already had a bearing and a voice that demanded attention.

Frank Bogert's arrival in Palm Springs may sound like the first draft of an old western movie, except it's true. And as this raw-boned wrangler will tell you, he was no tinsel-town cowboy who patted the girl and kissed the horse good-bye in the final scene.

Bogert ("that's Bo-GERT, not Bo-GART") was, and is, an unusual man. And, in a sense, is the personification of his city, Palm Springs.

At once friendly, cantankerous, warm, tough and witty, he projects his attitudes and beliefs with a conviction that can befuddle friend and foe alike. But, when they came up with the description "straight-arrow," someone probably had Bogert in mind.

Born New Year's Day of 1910 in Mesa, Colorado, Bogert was the youngest of eight children. His father drove cattle on the Grand Mesa and rode in Buffalo Bill Cody's Wild West Show. Bogert remembers that Butch Cassidy's hideout had been close to his family ranch. He told *The Desert Sun,* "Hell, everybody around there knew him. He was a nice guy."

His family moved to Los Angeles in 1923 and young Frank completed high school there. By then he had a string of horses that he rented out in summer. He kept them stabled north of San Bernardino. "It was too cold to rent them in the mountains in winter so I took 'em down to the desert," he recalls. "I set up a stable on the reservation and hired an old guy to run it. I had just started college at UCLA and every week-end I'd work the stable and on Monday run back to classes."

As youngsters on the range, Bogert and his brother, Charles, came to share an interest in reptiles and other desert creatures. At UCLA, he

Palm Springs "Cowboy Mayor" Frank Bogert is being honored by a five-ton, larger-than-life bronze statue in front of city hall. The sculpture is based on the above early photograph by his late friend Dick Wittington.

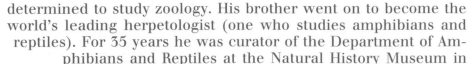

determined to study zoology. His brother went on to become the world's leading herpetologist (one who studies amphibians and reptiles). For 35 years he was curator of the Department of Amphibians and Reptiles at the Natural History Museum in New York.

By 1930, Bogert had 150 horses in his stables. "And during the depression, it was tough just keeping them in hay. So I sold most of them, took my camera and went to work promoting El Mirador. They were looking for some publicity and thought I was a pretty good photographer so I bought an old Speed Graphic and went to work," Bogert says.

During the winter tourist season, he took photos of visitors riding, swimming or just relaxing and mailed them off to home town newspapers and magazines. In summer, he'd travel putting on a cowboy roping and whip act and promoting Palm Springs by showing a movie.

When the Palm Springs Chamber of Commerce was formed in 1934, Bogert became its first manager. Later, he took a turn at managing Charlie Farrell's Racquet Club. But he never lost his love for riding. "I used to ride bucking horses and bulls. Finally, I decided that had no future for me, so I started announcing. I announced rodeos all over—in Reno, Tucson, Fresno, San Francisco, even in Mexico.

"I loved Mexico," he said, "still do. I'm kind of famous in Mexico because I'm one of the first gringo cowboys to be a Charro." Charros are an elite group of gentlemen riders who study and practice early style riding and roping. He learned the history and ways of the country and the Mexican people. Bogert beams when he tells of being called "El Grandote," the Tall One, by his Mexican admirers. They honored him with The Golden Spur Award, the highest given a Charro.

Like many his age, World War II put a twist in Bogert's path. Shortly after Pearl Harbor, he enlisted in the Navy. He reached the rank of lieutenant commander and became an admiral's aide. "I was an important son of a bitch," he laughs. When peace returned, Bogert headed back to Palm Springs and opened a dude ranch. He then joined two friends in starting an advertising and public relations firm. In 1958, he was elected to the City Council, and his fellow council members elected him mayor eight years in a row. In 1966, he resigned as mayor when his firm was bidding for a city contract.

For 15 years after he left office, Bogert and his associates ran a successful publicity agency. They also formed a company to run "Cabla-

Frank Bogert, among his many other accomplishments, has written a history of Palm Springs' first century.

gata," a Spanish term for people riding together. These rides were held all over the world. "We put on twelve in Mexico. We've had 'em in Spain, Portugal, Hawaii, even Africa," he said.

"By 1982, I didn't like the way things were going in the city. Everyone was fighting. The council wasn't doing anything. I felt like the downtown was finally going to hell. Everyone was pushing 'no growth' and I decided someone, like me, had to go in and shake things up."

And shake things, he did. From then until 1988, as Palm Springs' first directly elected mayor, he led the push for the revitalization of the city.

A *Desert Sun* article about Bogert said in the mid-1980s:

"A cantankerous cowboy who refers to women as 'fillies,' rides a horse with an unmentionable name and whose colorful language has left more than one resident blushing, holds the reins to America's most glamorous desert resort...He's a diamond in the rough who is as comfortable entertaining royalty as he is joking with the trashman...he rules Palm Springs with a combination of salty humor and common sense that has made him one of the most popular mayors in [the city's] history."

When asked what he had left undone in his final term as mayor, which ended in 1988, the still-feisty former cowboy pointed across the city and shot back, "Nothing! I got everything done I wanted to do. We wanted the Convention Center and we got it. I worked for 25 years to complete the Tahquitz Flood Control Project and we now have that. The Wyndham Hotel, Maxim's Hotel, the Desert Fashion Plaza: We got all of that done. We put in five new bridges, fixed up the airport and completed the cogeneration plants. My work's done."

Bogert, cowboy-publicist-developer-politician, summed up his full life in his own brusque manner: "I've had some good dogs, some good horses and some good women. If I die tomorrow, I'll have no regrets."

A new home for the Desert Sun *newspaper opened on Gene Autry Drive in 1989.*

CHAPTER FIVE

Palm Springs' image is

that of an exciting, exotic

FANTASY UPDATE

playground around the cal-

endar.

Palm Springs is maybe the one place where getting there is not part of the fun—you just want to get there. Now!...Why is it the one place on the entire planet where Mr. Frank Sinatra, with his tons and tons of money, chooses to live?

WESTERN LIVING MAGAZINE

At some point, Palm Springs stopped being a real place and became a fantasy of the good life impeccably lived.
TRAVEL & LEISURE MAGAZINE

Today's job is to make Palm Springs the fantasy that it is!
PALM SPRINGS MAYOR SONNY BONO, 1989

I n 1988, Palm Springs threw a party, and *everybody* showed up!

The occasion was the City's Golden Anniversary, its 50th birthday. For six months, November to April, the celebrations held a little—or a lot—for everyone.

The massive gala was kicked off by a huge parade with Ralph Bellamy as grand marshal. Floats and bands and marching Marines, along with more than 3,000 children, strutted in the golden glow of Palm Canyon Drive. Events during the day ranged from appearances by Mexican singing Charros to the marching of Scottish bagpipers.

Banners with a 50th Anniversary logo bedecked the palm-lined thoroughfare. A set of commemorative coins was struck. And lyricist Buddy Kaye and musician Phil Moody collaborated in writing a birthday song, "My Town Is Palm Springs." In February, a reception opened the new $68 million, 410-room Wyndham Hotel on the two-mile strip from downtown-center to the newly renovated airport. An evening event also christened the new 100,000-square-foot Palm Springs Convention Center.

Year-long festivities hit their peak during "Golden Week" in April. At a day-long party in Sunrise Park, masses of people were fed, entertained

A stellar gathering at the McCallum Theater for the Performing Arts. Left to right: Vic Damone, Mel Torme, Frank and Barbara Sinatra, Diane Schuur, Roger Moore and Peter Nero.

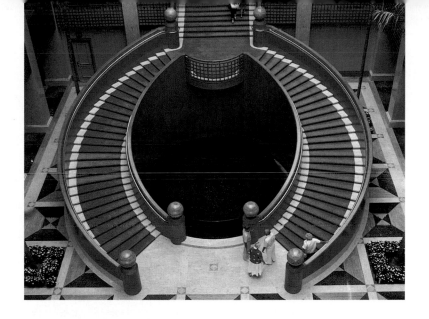

Above: *Clubhouse at The Vintage Club, exclusive resort in Indian Wells.*
Top: *Grand staircase in the foyer of the Esmeralda Hotel in Indian Wells, which opened in November 1989.*

Palm Springs remains an

oasis of tranquility in the

desert, luring city dwellers

from Los Angeles and Lon-

don, Tokyo and Toronto.

and congratulated by local political leaders. For the kids, there were mimes, puppets and jugglers, and even an elephant ride. That evening, as the gigantic helium-filled balloons for the Gordon Bennett Race lifted against a full moon, Palm Springs buried a time capsule, not to be opened until 2038—the City's Centennial.

Today, Palm Springs remains an oasis of tranquility for stressed-out city dwellers. From Los Angeles and London, from Tokyo to Toronto, visitors are lured to this "Shangri-La" in the desert. And leading the city's day-by-day parade of progress is Mayor Sonny Bono.

Yes! That Sonny Bono.

Elected in a landslide victory in the closing days of the Golden Birthday Party, Bono is spearheading a drive to revitalize and maintain the city's international reputation as a world-class resort, as well as a residential community.

Attempting to mollify the diverse interests of the city's old guard and the avant-garde with everything from community coffee klatsches to an international film festival, Palm Springs' 16th mayor has his work cut out for him. "The old guard are the backbone of the city," he believes. "They are the people who pioneered this town. They had the dream and did so much. They were the movers and shakers."

"I had an exterior point of view," Bono explains. "When you come into a deal fresh, your dreams may be more naive, but they are also more exciting, sometimes."

So Palm Springs continues to polish its image as an exciting, exotic playground around the calendar. As if natural wonders and available vacation amenities were not enough, the city has initiated a string of special events to attract even the staunchest workaholics out of the office:

• **BicycleMania:** In October, Palm Springs welcomes a pack of the world's leading individual and team cyclists to "the season's" first event. In this international three-day attraction, separate times are set for recreational cyclist fun rides, freestyle stunt competitions, a "human-powered vehicle" race, and a sports and fitness expo.

• In November, the **Palm Springs Sports Festival** is held. Celebrities,

Left: Palm Springs Aerial Tramway shuttles 400,000 visitors annually to the 8,500-foot San Jacinto.
Right: At 1989's first annual running of BicycleMania.

Opened in 1988, the Palm Springs Convention Center is adjacent to the equally-new Wyndham Hotel, just a short distance from the city center.

On Frank Sinatra Drive in Rancho Mirage, a $1-million fountain greets guests at the entrance to the Ritz-Carlton Hotel.

amateurs and professional athletes compete in a festival atmosphere. This is conducted in conjunction with the Veteran's Day Relay Marathon, a classic golf tournament and celebrity tennis match.

• The checkered flag begins the **Vintage Grand Prix** in Palm Springs in mid-November. This racing event on the city streets features world-recognized drivers in some of the finest driving machines made before 1969. The televised, nine-day event includes a multimillion-dollar **Concours d'Elegance** showcasing unique motor cars from around the world,

and parties and parades, as well as special driving events.

• Premiering in January 1990, the five-day **International Film Festival** includes films, parties and special events by the American Film Institute at several venues around town.

• Seeking a positive outlet for the thousands of exuberant college students who converge on Palm Springs during their annual spring break in April, **Spring Games U.S.A.** offers a healthy alternative Olympic competition format. Winners in the several athletic events meet with other winners for a final match-off in Ruth Hardy Park.

• A nine-day **Palm Springs Music Festival** is staged at six locations around the city at the end of April, featuring both indoor and outdoor performances. Classical, western, jazz, rock, swing, etc.—the multi-day festival will have them all.

• Held on the weekend closest to the full moon in late April or early May

Above left: Each November, the Avanti Palm Springs Vintage Grand Prix and Concours d'Elegance takes place on the streets of Palm Springs. The original Avanti was developed here in 1962.
Right: Classic-auto meets and auctions are held throughout the year in the desert resort communities.

each year, the **Gordon Bennett Balloon Race** brings more than 20,000 enthusiasts to Palm Springs each year. Launched at night from Ruth Hardy Park, internationally sanctioned helium balloons follow the winds to fly the longest distance without touching ground. Begun in Europe in 1906, this race has been held in six countries and, for the last decade, in California.

These events are just the icing on the Palm Springs cake. Everyday attractions include eight golf courses, the wondrous Indian Canyons, Desert Museum, Oasis Water Resort, Aerial Tramway, Village Green, Moorten's Botanical Gardens and, give or take a few, 10,000 palm trees—on city property alone!

Calbraith Perry Rodgers would be most impressed by the airport service now in Palm Springs. When Rodgers flew his "Vin Fizz Flyer" over Palm Springs in 1911, on the first U.S. transcontinental flight, all he probably saw (he flew at 2,000 feet) were some dusty roads, a few palm trees and Nellie sweeping her boardinghouse porch.

To handle the more than 825,000 people that use the Palm Springs Regional Airport annually, a $33.7 million expansion has been proposed. It is expected that the airport, now called "America's Resortport," will gear up to handle some 1.6 million annual passengers by the year 2010.

Al Smoot, airport director of aviation, counts eight airlines cur-

(continued on page 68)

Above left: America's "Resortport" began a major expansion program in 1989. It expects more than a million and a half passengers annually by the year 2010.

REGULA'S RACE

Regula Hug-Messner made a wish. When she was 10, her father won the Gordon Bennett Balloon Race in Paris. And Regula wished, one day, she could win it too.

The May morning, a few years ago, when Regula raced in the "GBBR" in Palm Springs, the day dawned cool and slightly windy. As the sun rose, however, the winds subsided and Regula soared aloft in competition against five international teams.

But trouble was on board that day. Regula recalled: "Nothing worked. The radio was dead and that night it was pitch black and cold." Then an unexpected weather front forced her into a crash landing in the mountains near Salt Lake City.

It wasn't until daybreak that Regula found she had flown as high as 14,000 feet and covered 525.6 miles in her rugged flight from Palm Springs.

At age 68, Regula's wish came true. She won her race.

Above: Regula Hug-Messner checks out her balloon prior to the Gordon Bennett International Balloon Race in Palm Springs.

Each year in April or May on the weekend closest to the full moon, the Gordon Bennett International Balloon Race is held from Palm Springs. The balloonists use the moonlight for their long-distance nighttime flights.

GEORGE SERVICE

rently flying 32 daily flights to connectors with major cities. There are also more than 50 daily commuter flights to Los Angeles, Phoenix and Las Vegas.

A $3.5 million facelift, first step in the airport's renovation, was completed in 1989. "We've added three new entrances, tripled curb space, and more than doubled the parking area," Smoot says. "And for the 'snowbirds' that can't leave their work in the office, we've installed a 'pay-as-you-use-it' FAX machine in the terminal."

Next in the "Resortport's" future will be, when funding is approved, an expanded terminal complex and a new 4,970-foot runway for small aircraft. It will parallel Runway 12-30, the airport's 8,500-foot primary strip for large, commercial flights.

In addition to the main airport, two fixed-base operations, Jimsair and AMR Combs, service and fuel about another 25,000 corporate and private flights per year. Even here the Palm Springs flair shines through: At Jimsair, a swimming pool and spa await weary pilots.

Each year for the past decade, an average of 135,000 people have gathered in Palm Springs for conventions of all kinds: business, military, trade and even a "Rock-Around-the-Clock" New Year's Eve party. Since last year, they meet in Palm Springs' new 100,000-square-foot convention center. This unconventional center for conventions is just three blocks from Palm Canyon Drive, the Desert Fashion Plaza and Maxim's de Paris Suite Hotel. Around the corner is The

Ocotillo in blossom in Cottonwood Canyon, Joshua Tree National Monument.

Marquis Hotel, and connected directly to it, by covered walkway, is the equally new Wyndham Hotel.

While there are more than 7,000 available rooms in Palm Springs, only 14 hotels have more than 150 rooms. About 130, or 80 percent of the hotels in Palm Springs, have fewer than 50 rooms. A 1989 issue of *Palm Springs Life* magazine determined that "Today, perhaps because of a nostalgia for the charm and slower pace of days gone by, there is renewed hunger for lodgings that cry cozy, quaint and private." For example, at the Casa Cody, a small, historic spot, tucked in behind busy Palm Canyon Drive, co-owner Frank Tysen tells of "one lovely lady who arrives every year with her husband, who attends a major convention. She told her husband, 'I don't like those big places with guys in black suits and shiny badges. I'll stay here and you come visit me. It's cozy that way'." With only 17 units, Casa Cody exemplifies those small hotels that have formed the Small Discoveries Association of Palm Springs.

While one small hotel may offer wine and cheese at poolside, or breakfast in bed served by an English-trained butler, others will whisk you away for tee-time or tea-time in a vintage Rolls Royce.

Whether your choice runs to large or small accommodations, when you check out you will pay a "transient occupancy tax." While small on each individual bill, by year's end it brings some $5.8 million into the city's coffers. With

Top: One of the more than 30 dining spots along "Restaurant Row," Rancho Mirage. Cuisines of many nations are available.
Bottom: *Large and small shops and restaurants can be found on El Paseo in Palm Desert.*

The Palm Springs Desert Museum offers art and natural science exhibits—ranging from an extensive American Indian artifacts collection to changing art exhibits—in its 75,000-square-foot, split-level structure.

TERRY O'NEILL

these funds, of course, Palm Springs will continue to focus on cultivating its resort capabilities.

Assessed valuation in the city has surpassed $3 billion—not bad for a confined community that sold building lots for $45 each a century ago. Today, of course, many of these same lots are valued at $700,000. And taxable retail sales each year are in the neighborhood of $450 million. Nice neighborhood.

At this writing, Palm Springs' Plaza de Las Flores nears completion. Right in the heart of downtown, on the original site of Miss Cornelia's house, this complex includes retail and commercial space. And on the planning list is a major concert and entertainment center—with, perhaps, a pari-mutuel horse racing track and world-class golf. These would be located just east of the airport on a 1,000-acre site that, as some developers wish, would be linked to downtown by a tunnel under the airport itself.

"Judge" McCallum started the Palm Springs fantasy. Fortunately, it came true...and continues.

COACHELLA VALLEY BY THE NUMBERS

POPULATION PROJECTION

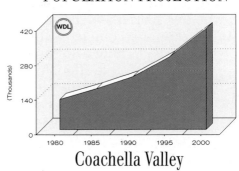

Coachella Valley

ACCOMMODATIONS
Coachella Valley's largest resorts, in numbers of rooms available, 1988:

891 MARRIOTT'S DESERT SPRINGS, Palm Desert

605 LA QUINTA HOTEL GOLF AND TENNIS RESORT, La Quinta

560 STOUFFER ESMERALDA RESORT, Indian Wells

475 RADISSON PALM SPRINGS RESORT, Palm Springs

456 MARRIOTT'S RANCHO LAS PALMAS RESORT, Rancho Mirage

ANNUAL HOTEL ROOM SALES

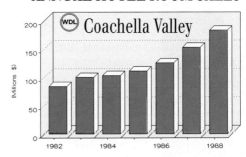

GROWTH IN TAXABLE SALES

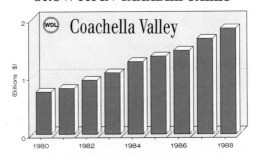

TOTAL TAXABLE SALES

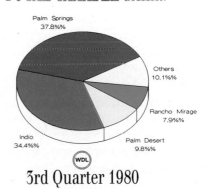

3rd Quarter 1980

TOTAL TAXABLE SALES

3rd Quarter 1988

DIAGRAMS COURTESY OF WHEELER'S DESERT LETTER

The economy of the Coachella Valley is growing rapidly. But, more and more, the rapid expansion is in the newer cities that have room available for development.

"I GOT YOU, BABE!"

"I suppose I have to wear a tie and coat?" was Mayor Bono's lament when informed by his secretary, Mary Martin, that he had a news conference the following morning. Ms. Martin, who has served as secretary to every Palm Springs mayor for 23 years, simply reminded him of the time and who would be in attendance. While loose-fitting shirts and cotton pants are, no doubt, his personal choice, Mayor Bono can play many roles.

Born into a Sicilian-American family in Detroit, he moved with his parents to Los Angeles at age seven. His mother's and father's wish that he be a doctor couldn't shake *his* wish to be in show business.

COURTESY CITY OF PALM SPRINGS

Perhaps his first brush with controversy occurred as a high school senior. He brought the first black singing group into the school (a move not condoned at that time) and was suspended for three days.

His professional career in musical entertainment began at Dig Records, when he was 17. The Righteous Brothers' hit "Koko Joe" won his first songwriting award. But many more followed quickly. Within a decade, he had written five songs that reached the *Billboard* Top 100 chart, an achievement equalled only by the Beatles. Bono went on to become one of America's leading entertainers in the 1960s and 1970s. His first big success was the song "Needles and Pins," written in collaboration for Jackie de Shannon.

In 1964, with a borrowed $175, Bono teamed with his girlfriend, Cher Sarkisian, and released "Baby Don't Go." It went to the top of the charts

72

Sonny Bono and his wife, Mary, with their year-old son Chesare Elan Bono at their home in the Mesa area of Palm Springs.

and was followed by "I Got You, Babe," "Bang Bang" and "The Beat Goes On." The Sonny and Cher duo resulted in 10 gold records, all songs written by Bono.

Controversy reared up again when, in the late 1960s, both Sonny and Cher were among the first pop singers to come out publicly against drugs—the hip set shot them down. It was then they reformatted their act, with Bono becoming the foil for Cher's put-down jokes. This drew them a replacement slot on TV. The "Sonny and Cher Show" was a quick success and received top ratings until the act broke up in 1974.

A guest actor on many TV shows, Bono also expanded his activity in feature films, such as "Escape to Athens" and "Airplane II." Early in the 1980s, he opened his first "Bono" restaurant in Hollywood. A second in Houston opened soon after. His "Bono's" restaurant in Palm Springs

When Palm Springs threw itself a birthday party in 1988, it didn't stint on any aspect of decorations or events for children of all ages.

"I have great visions for

Palm Springs...to become

the fantasy that it is."

replaced the earlier two and brought still more success but also brought him face to face with politics. His personal and professional run-ins with civic leaders led to his interest in Palm Springs government.

"I've always followed the yellow brick road," Bono quipped. "For me to run for mayor was a real left turn in the road. But I felt strongly, very strongly, that Palm Springs had so much potential that hadn't been tapped." He added, "Coming here for so long, I have great visions for Palm Springs. I think it must work to become the fantasy that it is. And I think I can channel the flow to make that happen."

Downtown Palm Springs is the center of his attention. Bono is acutely aware that the city has filled its available space. "We have to capitalize our assets and our biggest asset is downtown," he said. "It's had the same face for so many years, we need to take and reshape it. We need to make it the interesting tourist attraction it can be. I think what Palm Springs can be, should be, is an American Saint-Tropez or Monte Carlo."

So after years in television, radio, stage and movies, what does Bono think of his $15,000-a-year job as Mayor of Palm Springs? "I have days," he said, "when I think this is the worst job in the world. But then the very next day, it's so rewarding. I enjoy it. It's a real challenge. And I think with perseverance Palm Springs' continued success will be inevitable."

Above: Guests travel from lobby to rooms by boat at the Marriott Desert Springs Resort in Palm Desert.
Facing page: Palm Canyon. GEORGE SERVICE

CHAPTER SIX

Each desert resort commu-

nity has its individual style.

"DOWN VALLEY" NO MORE

I talk about our 70 golf courses, which are located "down valley," and the "down valley" promoters talk about their museum, water park and canyons, which, of course, are in Palm Springs. If we all talk as one and quit fighting each other, the whole valley will do well.

PALM SPRINGS MAYOR FRANK BOGERT—1987

After nearly three years of planning, the seven cities in the greater Palm Springs area—Palm Springs, Cathedral City, Rancho Mirage, Palm Desert, Indian Wells, La Quinta and Indio—have established a valley-wide convention and visitors bureau.

THE PALM SPRINGS DESERT RESORTS
CONVENTION & VISITORS BUREAU—JULY 1989

Syzygy, n.: the combined gravitational pull of celestial bodies configured in a nearly straight line.

WEBSTER'S COLLEGIATE DICTIONARY

Syzygy seems a silly word, but better than any other it describes what is happening to the Coachella Valley's tourism-driven economy.

When Palm Springs took on star status as the celebrities' sandbox of choice in the first half of the century, the rest of the valley remained in its shadow. The six major contiguous communities stretching southeast from Palm Springs toward the Salton Sea have been collectively, and somewhat disparagingly, referred to as "down valley." Admittedly, as the valley' eastern end reaches sea level, each city is, in a sense, "down" from the other. However, in recent years, development has levelled the tourism playing field, putting these rapidly growing cities on a more equal footing with Palm Springs. They are down valley no more.

Above: *Luncheon at the Palm Valley Country Club, one of the scores of desert dining spots in the "down valley" communities.*
Facing page: *Sand verbena and desert sun flowers at Edom Hill north of Interstate 10.*
GEORGE SERVICE

VALLEY TALK
A GLOSSARY

Many of the names in the Coachella Valley have come from Spanish or Indian words. Accordingly, they don't always sound the way you might expect them to. Here are some of the more often mispronounced valley words, along with a phonetic guide:

Ajo.........AH - ho
Avenida........ah - veh - NE - dah
Borrego........boar - EH- go
Cabelleros........kah - bah - YAIR - os
Cahuilla........kah - WEE - ah
Calle........KAH - yea
Cholla........CHOY - ah
Cielo........sce - EH - low
Jacinto........ha - SIN - toe
LaQuinta........lah - KEEN - tah
Mohave........moe - HA - veh
Olla........OY - ah
Ramon........rah - MOAN
Taquitz........TAH - quits (or) TAH - quiz

Above: From mariachi music to jazz and opera to country-western, music of many choices is heard in the Coachella Valley.

Facing page: Individual homes seem to be the direction of the future in the resort communities. For many years a location for only vacation homes and condominiums, the area now has more families who are year-round residents.

While all the cities in the desert resort area share several things in common, such as unbeatable weather and some of the world's finest recreational facilities and unparalleled amenities, they are also diverse. Today, although they pursue their separate development plans and schedules, they are now pulling together like a tug-rope team to lure tourists to the area. That's syzygy and it's working.

After years of controversy and three years of planning, the desert resort communities now have banded together and funded a "Palm Springs Desert Resorts Convention and Visitors Bureau." Established in 1989, with an annual budget of $1.6 million and 19 employees, this organization, in effect, eliminates the valley-wide competition and enables the seven cities to have a single voice in approaching the domestic and international convention and tourism marketplace.

Like horses from a starting gate, however, each of Palm Springs' six sister cities began at a different pace.

CATHEDRAL CITY
Depending on which story you prefer, this fast-growing city, which bumps elbows with the eastern edge of Palm Springs, was named for either a nearby rock formation or a canyon in the San Jacinto Mountains because the city has no real cathedral.

In 1850, an Army engineer on survey duty noted a deep canyon in the area which appeared to him to resemble a cathedral. He scrawled "Cathedral Canyon" on his map. Aggressive developers in 1925 dubbed the area's first sub-division Cathedral City. Two years later, the old Bradshaw stagecoach trail was paved as a state road and retail business began.

In the mid-1930s to 1940s, Cathedral City gained notoriety for its three

"Golf Capital of the World" is a title well deserved by the Coachella Valley. More than 70 courses host more than 100 tournaments each year.

illegal gambling casinos, The Dunes, The 139 Club and The Cove Club, which catered to guests from the El Mirador and The Desert Inn in Palm Springs. As law enforcement strengthened and clientele changed, gambling disappeared in the valley. Today, however, there is again controversy in Cathedral City about a proposed "card club." Whether gambling will return this time is up to resident voters.

Incorporated in 1981 as the City of Cathedral City (and some residents still cringe at the legalistic redundancy), the area selected as its motto "A City in Perfect Balance." And, indeed, that's true.

Unlike the other valley cities, it has a diverse base of light industry, an immense automall with 13 dealerships, several large major discount stores and a concentration of small retail shops and restaurants to serve its 27,000 residents.

Swimming and just relaxing in the sun still are prime attractions in the desert resorts. The unofficial count puts more than 7,000 pools in the Coachella Valley.

81

Like Central Park in New York, the Cathedral Canyon Country Club is a tranquil gated complex almost surrounded by the city's busy thoroughfares. The club's 1,000 homes and condos wind through a championship 18-hole golf course, a 10-court tennis center and club house. The adjoining Cathedral Canyon Resort hotel is annual host to the Desert Dixieland Jazz Festival. The city proclaims itself "Jazz Capital of the Sunny Desert."

At the north end of the city is the $120 million Desert Princess Hotel and Country Club, now operated by Doubletree Resorts. Opened in 1985, this 385-acre complex has more than 1,000 condominium units, an 18-hole golf course and a variety of swimming, tennis and racquetball facilities.

RANCHO MIRAGE

Known as the "Playground of Presidents," this exclusive community is home to about 9,000 people. Among them are former President Gerald R. Ford, Ambassador Walter Annenburg, entertainer Dinah Shore and Mr. and Mrs. Francis Albert Sinatra.

Originally called Eleven Mile Ranch in 1924 because of its location 11 miles to both Palm Springs and Indio, this section of the desert was one of the early date palm groves in the valley. There was little else here until E.L. "Hank" Gogerty built an airstrip in 1945, called Mirage Airpark. (A Los Angeles real estate salesman had garbled his French and Spanish idioms to coin the name "Rancho Mirage.")

Gogerty's airpark expanded to become the Desert Air Hotel, an out-of-the-way facility with a grass runway. It was frequented mostly by private pilots from the movie industry as a hideaway to dine and relax. That same year, the Thunderbird Country Club was started nearby. Other clubs followed quickly and Rancho Mirage incorporated as a city in 1973.

Today, Rancho Mirage is home to the internationally known Eisenhower Medical Center. Dedicated in 1971 by the former President and Mrs. Eisenhower, the center was built on 80 acres of land donated by Bob Hope and his wife, Dolores. Included in this institution is the Betty Ford Center, founded by the former First Lady, for treatment of alcoholism and other chemical dependencies. Another facility is the Barbara Sinatra Children's Center, which provides outpatient psychological services for abused children. Adjoining the medical center is the world famous Heart Institute of the Desert.

Marriott Hotels introduced their Rancho Las Palmas Resort in Rancho Mirage in 1979. The Mission Hills Resort, now annual host to the Nabisco-Dinah Shore Championship Golf Tournament, opened in mid-1980.

Above: The Eisenhower Medical Center in Rancho Mirage is largest of the valley's three key medical facilities. Desert Hospital in Palm Springs and John F. Kennedy Hospital in Indio also are expanding.

Facing page: Moorish-style architecture blends well into the desert scene. This entry to the Westin Mission Hills Resort in Rancho Mirage looks toward the Little San Bernardino Mountains.

High on a hillside overlooking the valley, the Ritz Carlton Rancho Mirage Resort opened on Frank Sinatra Drive in 1988. This 24-acre hotel and tennis facility is the focal point for the larger, but just as ritzy, Mirada residential development.

Directly below this newest Rancho Mirage resort is Restaurant Row, which stretches the width of the city, offering some 30 dining choices.

For its future, Rancho Mirage is planning Plaza Mirage, a 27-acre downtown project off Highway 111. It is envisioned to include offices, stores, art galleries, an amphitheater and possibly a civic center complex. The vivid need for expanded city office facilities was dramatized in 1989 when officials parked a leased trailer in their parking lot as a temporary office for the growing government staff.

PALM DESERT

When General George S. Patton's tanks broke down during desert training exercises in the early 1940s, they were repaired at his 3rd Army Tank Base in what is today Palm Desert. Before that the area held little more than a few scattered homesteads and a road over its alluvial fan up into the cooler mountain regions.

After the war, Palm Valley, as it was then known, told Los Angeles investors, "No other community in America offers the unique advantages of Palm Valley." That may, or may not, have been totally true then. But it sure is today.

Linchpin to the valley, with three cities to either side, Palm Desert tried to become a city a half-dozen times in the 1950s and 1960s but voters

85

Above: With its unique "figure-8" pool and tennis complex, Shadow Mountain resort, one of the earliest desert vacation spots, is annual host to a series of major tennis tournaments.
Facing page, top: Packed away behind foliage and gates, many smaller resorts such as Desert Island seldom are seen except from the air.
Bottom: College of the Desert is a focal point in Palm Desert. The McCallum Theater at the Bob Hope Cultural Center adjoins the college campus.

turned down the idea. Incorporation was finally achieved in 1973. "We worked out a design that would maintain the integrity of the desert through controlled growth and emphasis on the quality of living," recalls Hank Clark, the city's first mayor.

Shadow Mountain Resort, first with its man-made boating pond and later its large and unusual figure-8 swimming pool, was the first Palm Desert vacation spot in 1948. The opening of College of the Desert 14 years later was another milestone in the city's history.

Since it became a full-fledged city, Palm Desert has expanded to 16 square miles from its original eight. Today its population of almost 20,000 is growing between five and 10 percent each year.

As it has vied with Palm Springs for tourists since the 1950s, Palm Desert, perhaps more than any other city on the Highway 111 picket line, has been responsible for the valley's growth. There it isn't a question of finding something to do; the problem is, more likely, what to do next.

Palm Desert has become the retail hub of the desert resort area. El Paseo, a 1.8-mile arc through its mid-section, is known as "Rodeo Drive of the Desert." Across Highway 111, the Palm Desert Town Center, with its 140 shops, a 160-foot ice skating rink, movie theaters, four major department stores and multiple restaurants, is the largest shopping mall in the valley.

To date, the largest resort in the valley is the 900-room Desert Springs Resort and

PALM SPRINGS HISTORICAL SOCIETY

Lest any spies get the idea General Patton's troops were training with trucks in the Coachella Valley, this obviously constructed WWII-era photograph portrayed a mass of men and (somewhat outdated) equipment here.

Spa, a Marriott development in Palm Desert. With a chain of lakes and lagoons that culminates in its lobby, and a U.S. Coast Guard-approved passenger vessel for guests, this $300-million mega-resort was recently described in the *Los Angeles Times*:

"Fish the size of small sharks dart through the lagoon and a player piano turns out ragtime tunes. It's obvious this is not the little desert inn Hollywood once idolized. Indeed, [this] is a showplace with a dozen restaurants and snack bars serving everything from sushi to steak tartare...Swans cruise alongside flamingos and flamingos cruise past three swimming pools, one with a white sand beach. Doormen gussied up like French Foreign Legionnaires lend a hand at the door and airport arrivals are picked up by limousine."

Eight country clubs and resorts in Palm Desert offer visitors some of the best golf in the valley. There are also the unusual Living Desert reserve and Aerie Sculpture Garden to tour. But the crown jewel in the city is the 1,166-seat McCallum Theater for the Performing Arts in the new Bob Hope Cultural Center. Presenting leading symphonies, operas, touring companies, as well as dance, drama and personality performances, the 1988 McCallum Theater has scheduled everything from the London Symphony to Sarah Vaughn.

Planning for its guests has worked well for Palm Desert. So the city isn't stopping now. Seven new commercial developments south of Highway 111 are under consideration, along with ideas for the vast open land on

In the cove of Eisenhower Mountain adjacent to The Living Desert, Ironwood Country Club is just one of many of the valley's growing list of year-round golf complexes.

the north side of the city. And Disneyland—move aside: Palm Desert is now looking at a monorail system to decrease traffic congestion.

INDIAN WELLS

Picture, if you will, a lone, dusty cowboy stopping for a drink of cool water from a 30-foot well which had been hand-dug by Indian women uncounted years earlier.

Now see elegantly attired tourists on stunning, twin circular staircases at their luxury hotel.

One scene is the past; the other the present. Both are Indian Wells, a century apart.

Two markers on Highway 111, just east of Eldorado and behind the town hall, indicate the sites of the original wells that gave this city its name. For many years, this watering hole served Indians, then prospectors and stagecoach passengers and, eventually, the railroads.

Water in the desert meant life, food and just plain survival. In 1860, the California Legislature authorized $5,000 to dig wells here to facilitate a mail route to Arizona. A damp spot in the desert, Indian Wells remained an isolated agricultural area longer than most others in the area. It wasn't until the 1960s, when Palm Desert tried to acquire it, that the 285 local voters made it a city. Elected as its first mayor was Norris Goff (Goff had been "Abner" on the "Lum and Abner" radio show.)

The town had been formed a decade earlier from residential lots adjoining the new Indian Wells Country Club. Small even today in terms of population, with a little more than 2,000 year-round residents, Indian Wells thinks big—and grand.

GEORGE SERVICE

MARK THOMPSON

88

Above left: Bigelow cactus in Carrizo Canyon of the Santa Rosa Mountains.
Right: The private Vintage Club at Indian Wells hosts the annual Vintage-Chrysler Invitational for the world's top 54 golfers.

As an example, the Vintage Club, begun in 1979, is a 712-acre private, golf-oriented community. It includes 509 planned luxury residences, an 85,000-square-foot clubhouse and two 18-hole championship golf courses. Its Mountain Golf Course was selected by *Golf* magazine as one of the top 100 courses in the world. The Vintage-Chrysler Invitational, which draws 54 of the world's top golfers, is hosted here each year.

Across Highway 111, a pair of new resorts have risen. The Hyatt Grand Champions, with its 10,500-seat tennis stadium, is home to the annual Newsweek Cup Tournament, Virginia Slims Tournament and NCAA Tennis Finals. Sharing the same palm-lined entrance is Stouffer's Esmeralda, a $117-million complex opened in November 1989.

According to a historian,

Indian tribes once consid-

ered the La Quinta area site

of the "Garden of Eden,"

where life on earth began.

LA QUINTA

When early Spanish explorers traveled, they rode long and hard. For four days they would push on from before dawn until dark. On the fifth day—La Quinta—they would rest. In time, this term came to mean a resting place and then a small country estate.

Early in the 1920s, a wealthy San Franciscan built an exclusive hotel in a cove of the Santa Rosa Mountains, just west of Indio. He called it—La Quinta.

During the 1930s, Desert Club of La Quinta was built, primarily to promote building sites in the cove area. Later, a golf course and several homes went up near the original hotel and eventually grew in number to become La Quinta Country Club.

When the building boom struck the Coachella Valley in the 1970s, developers purchased hundreds of acres in La Quinta's 22-square-mile area. In 1982, to control its rapid growth, La Quinta incorporated as a city, and became the first recorded city to be named after a hotel.

Today this youngest of the desert resort cities has 8,000 residents and nine golf courses, four of which make up P.G.A. West, co-host each year to the Bob Hope Chrysler Classic and the "Skins" Game.

The La Quinta Hotel has completed a $4.5 million expansion and P.G.A. West is also adding to its facilities.

90

Styled after the early Spanish missions, St. Francis Church in La Quinta glows warmly in the early-morning sunlight.

"Faire a La Quinta," the city's annual arts festival, and its growing jazz festival have both become highly acclaimed events.

Cahuilla Indian historian Elizabeth Siva Sauvee said, "Ancient local tribes called La Quinta 'The Garden of Eden.' They believed it was the cradle of civilization where human life began on earth."

One of the fastest-growing sections of the valley is Santa Rosa Cove in La Quinta. Several new major resorts are planned in the area.

Known for its agriculture—

95 percent of America's

date crop grows here—

Indio is also the "Western

Polo Capital of the United

States."

INDIO

It seems there was one too many "Indian Wells" in the Coachella Valley in 1877. The Southern Pacific Railroad had begun service from Los Angeles to Indian Wells in May of the previous year. But just a bit west on the Bradshaw Trail was this other area, also called Indian Wells. To avoid confusion the one with the railroad station, now the oldest city in the valley, changed its name to Indio. As the Cabazon Indian Reservation was just south of the new rail station, the name seemed appropriate to all concerned.

In 1894, residents worked out plans for an Indio townsite. A general store and stables and corral were followed by a "tent" school and post office. Four years later, Cinderella Courtney arrived, the first non-Indian child to be born in the valley.

"At about the same time," said Palm Springs author Karen Minckler, "the seed from which Indio's future would grow was germinating in the minds of a handful of men. Until 1898, an American date industry was little more than a dream, although the concept had been explored as early as 1818. Lack of critical knowledge related to growing conditions and cultivation resulted in decades of frustration.

"The Coachella Valley," said Minckler, "did not celebrate its first off-shoot plantings until October 1903, due largely to the tenacity and persistence of date pioneer Bernard Johnson. By 1913, cooperative efforts formed the Coachella Valley Date Growers Association in Indio. Thus began the import shipments which were to become the foundation for date culture in the Coachella Valley and the United States."

COURTESY OF
SUNWORLD INTERNATIONAL

Ninety-five percent of America's date crop—27 million pounds annually—is now grown in this region. The National Date Festival has been held in Indio each year since 1921. In 1989 it attracted 250,000 visitors.

Today Indio still is known for its agriculture, which produces $240 million each year in dates, citrus, asparagus, grapes and other table crops. At the same time, it has become a major distribution point and retail center. The 250,000-square-foot Indio Fashion Mall is doubling in size and a 190,000-square-foot business park is under construction.

Each desert resort city, it seems, has a unique feature. In Indio it's polo. So popular has polo become in Indio that the Eldorado Polo Club has quadrupled its membership in a half dozen years. More than 125 players and 1,000 horses converge on the club each season. When the country's oldest polo tournament, the United States Polo Association Open, re-

Peppers, grapes, citrus fruits and more make the Coachella Valley one of America's highest-yield agricultural areas.

Ninety-five percent of America's date crop is grown in the Coachella Valley.

Of living in the Coachella

Valley, one resident said,

"There's no freeway hassle

nor smog here—and my

golf clubs are in the car."

turned to Indio in 1983, after a 21-year absence, the city was listed as "Western Polo Capital of the United States."

In 1989, the Empire Polo club opened in Indio on a 130-acre site that will accommodate 500 horses. Planned for completion in 1991, Empire will have three outdoor fields, two indoor fields, stables, barn, tack and veterinary facilities. And in keeping with other valley resorts, a lake, park, pavilion, hotel and condominiums will round out the club's amenities.

Desert resort visitors have easy access to the polo clubs. Indio officials say that due to arrangements between the clubs and hotels, visitors can reach matches via regularly-scheduled buses. And the grounds and viewing area for the matches are *free*.

In very few years, the cities of the desert resort area have grown from stagecoach stops to a budding metropolitan area.

But is bigger necessarily better?

One person who has seen both eras in the valley says maybe not. Barbara Moore, sister of Ted McKinney and the first white woman born in Palm Springs, recalls her mother's words: "If bigger were better, every family would have 12 children."

But at the rate the valley population is growing, it's starting to look like everyone had those dozen kids and they're all returning for a reunion.

According to *Wheeler's Desert Letter (WDL)*, which reports on such things, Riverside County is the fastest growing in California. Current county population is 1 million and is expected to expand by 37 percent by the year 2000. Coachella Valley's population exploded by 66 percent in the last decade to 202,000. And an additional 90,000 return every winter. By the year 2000, *WDL* expects this combined total to grow to 530,000—and that doesn't include tourists. With the number of new destination resort hotels popping up across the valley, the number of those vacationing and attending conventions also will escalate.

If nothing else changed, the almost uncontrolled growth in the numbers of those playing golf will assure the desert resorts' prosperity. Today, says *WDL*, 20 million Americans play golf and that will double in 10 years. That means the current $20-billion golf industry in the United States will

Indio is the "Western Polo Capital of the United States" and home to Eldorado and Empire Polo Clubs.

double to $40 billion by the year 2000.

With the new hotels, special events, added convention centers, and now the unified promotion by the joint Palm Springs Desert Resorts Convention and Visitors Bureau, the economy in the Coachella Valley has nowhere to go but up—and fast.

Continued growth of the combined resident and visitor base has sent total taxable and retail sales in the valley up about 150 percent since 1980. This is expected to continue climbing about eight to ten percent annually.

Of course, growth has its own problems. With all these new residents and their cars, transporta-

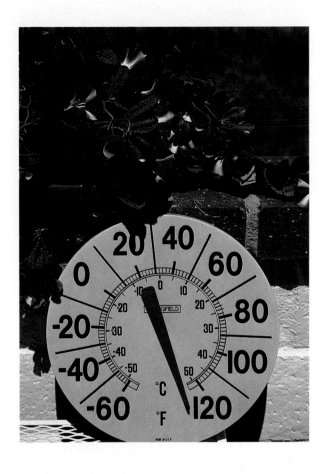

tion concerns arise. Growing families require homes, schools, health care and additional services. And the many thousands of people who will staff the present and future resorts will have the same needs.

Former Palm Springs Mayor Bogert pointed out that "all the valley cities are studying their master plans in an attempt to control growth. Densities are being cut back; building heights are limited with proper set backs, hillside projects are extremely limited and open space ordinances are being put into effect."

With such staggering mutual concerns and constraints by individual cities' parochial interests, an organization called the Coachella Valley Association of Governments has formed. Through this group, "member governments do things for themselves, together." CVAG, at it's known, is a forum to discuss regional problems and present solutions for the separate cities to work together in a coordinated manner.

More recently, another force called Coachella Valley Tomorrow has been established and funded by a diverse group of local businesses. In the belief that many existing jobs in the valley may be automated out of existence in the foreseeable future, this team is attempting to attract commercial and light-industrial firms to the valley to create new primary jobs.

While on the surface it may appear that the valley's single economic thrust is tourism, it does have another industry but tourists seldom see it—except on the end of a fork. It's agriculture.

The superb climate and excellent local management of water resources combine to let the valley produce the highest yield per irrigated

PHOTOS COURTESY OF SUNWORLD INTERNATIONAL

agricultural acre in the world. Located primarily from Indio southeast to the Salton Sea, some 70,000 acres in this region are turned from desert to fertile farmland by water received from the Colorado River by way of the All American Canal. Grapes and dates are the leading local crops but Coachella grapefruit, lemons, corn, alfalfa, tangerines, red potatoes and cotton also are produced in great quantity.

Riverside County is the agricultural leader in Southern California and almost one half its annual volume (or $331 million worth of crops) grows in the Coachella Valley. James O. Wallace, Riverside County agricultural commissioner, estimates that "every dollar received by farmers in 1988 had the financial impact of three times that amount." That means Coachella Valley's 1988 agricultural gross value of $331 million becomes $993 million—almost $1 billion. But here also the Coachella Valley

Above left: Almost $1 billion each year is the financial impact of agriculture in the desert resort area.
Above: More than 70,000 acres of the Coachella Valley became fertile farmland with the controlled irrigation available from the Colorado River.

Riverside County is Southern California's agricultural leader, with half of its $331 million in annual crops being grown in the Coachella Valley.

Tomorrow staff sees automation chipping away at primary jobs and the need for alternate opportunities for the valley's workforce.

Winds of change already are bringing new life to the valley's economy. "The lack of local suppliers was a major hurdle just a few years ago," recalled Charles "Chuck" Davis, who heads up his own advertising and marketing agency in Palm Desert. "With few local vendors, the pace of valley business was very slow. But in just a few years, more and more small businesses have opened up. Photographers, print shops, delivery services, automobile service centers are all now available year 'round. Discount markets, home supply outlets, medical offices and neighborhood restaurants are appearing up and across the valley as more families buy homes in the area." With a growing business in the desert resort area, Davis says the expanding local economy is a challenge but a nice one. And after 20 years in advertising in greater Los Angeles, he says, "There's no freeway hassle nor smog here—and my golf clubs are in the car."

Summarizing the valley's growth in a late-1980s *Palm Springs Life* magazine article called "Coachella Valley in the Year 2000," Fred Wolff, first mayor of La Quinta and former member of the CVAG executive board, said it well:

"The list of needs to address the growth of the valley over the next 13 years could go on and on. There is trash collection and supermarkets, golf carts and airports, utilities and restaurants, hospitals, day-care centers, dentists, preachers, morticians, auto repair, etc....

"But all these are part of the natural growth, and somehow supply meets demand. It's the marketplace of an open society.

"No doubt the Coachella Valley will remain a most desirable place to live and visit. Nature has provided this little spot on earth with unique physical endowments, which bring serenity and relaxation to those who inhabit it.

"Man has sought to develop a style of living for both residents and visitors that blends with the physical environment, enhancing the opportunities for 'the good life.'

"Hopefully, the tremendous growth of population during the coming years will be accommodated in such a manner that the attractions of the valley will be preserved. That requires the cooperation of political decisionmakers, developers and all citizens. It must be the primary goal of the years to come."

Rainbow Trout Center in Whitewater draws young and old from a wide area. A $2 tackle rental is the attraction's only fee.

CHAPTER SEVEN

The Valley offers diverse

things to see and do.

SUN AND SAND

G olf, of course, is 'flog' spelled backward," said Sam Howard, award-winning Cathedral Canyon Country Club pro. He thinks that may have given rise to the Coachella Valley legend that claims "in yesteryear early Indians were damned for beating the earth with sticks. It was called witchcraft. Today, tourists flog the ground, damn the sticks and call it—golf."

E ndless sunshine, clean, dry air and some of the world's finest golf courses, polo fields and tennis courts await the arrival of the more than 4 million people who are welcomed yearly to the desert resorts. But beyond even these, the "Playground of the Stars" abounds with diverse things to do, see and experience. From "undeserty" activities like ice-skating and salt-water fishing to sports, nature and man-made attractions, there is something to fit the fantasies of all who come here.

By day, there are shopping choices between haute couture and California casual at elegant boutiques along El Paseo in Palm Desert. More than 100 galleries, shops and designer-label establishments in the Palm Springs Desert Fashion Plaza tempt tourists with selections ranging from tuxedo studs and pearls to toddler's toys and chocolate chip cookies. In the middle of the valley, Palm Desert Town Center's 140 specialty stores serve up selections from the ever-present tourist tee-shirt to the finest in evening wear.

When the sun goes down and the sand begins to cool, the desert's night lights begin to sparkle. Whether you select one of the more than 30 award-winning dining choices along "Restaurant Row" in Rancho Mirage or a sidewalk cafe in Palm Springs, you can find almost any menu you wish in the valley. From hotel dining rooms to country hideaways, from fast food to candle-light dinners, the choice is yours.

Later, whether it's screaming guitars or delightful divas, classic or current comedy, dancing or just conversation, the desert resort area offers all these and more to light up the nights.

Local tourist directories present literally hundreds of places, events and attractions to choose from. Here is a brief look at valley highlights.

Above: The 21-acre Oasis Water Park in Palm Springs has the largest wave pool in California.
Facing page: Upper Palm Canyon Falls area is in a remote section usually not seen by tourists. GEORGE SERVICE

SPORTS

GOLFING California's Coachella Valley was born of earthquakes, oceans and winds but its future may well hang on the lip of a 4.25-inch-hole in the ground and a simple, dimpled 1.62-ounce-sphere.

Acclaimed "Golf Capital of the World," the California resort area guards its crown closely. Golf courses dot the buff-toned desert like emeralds sprinkled in a bowl of brown sugar. Since oilman Tom O'Donnell designed his course behind the Desert Inn in 1930, more than 70 public, private and semi-private clubs have evolved as an almost-irresistible challenge to the world's leading linksters. The desert resorts offer hackers, duffers, intermediates and pros alike more than 100 tournaments to choose from around the calendar.

In O'Donnell's era, laying out a golf course was much simpler. If legend is correct, he purchased a site from Nellie Coffman and then laid out each of the nine holes on his private course by the distance he could hit with each of his clubs.

"The Palm Springs Invitational" in 1936, on the O'Donnell course, is believed to be the first golf tournament in the valley. Ten years later, Frank Bogert gathered a group of San Francisco investors together and purchased 633 acres of "down-valley" property for $34,000. They opened the Thunderbird Dude Ranch that was soon to make golfing history. (In 1930, the previous owner had paid $3,000 for the land.)

When Thunderbird opened in February 1951, it had the first 18-hole golf course in the valley and green fees were $1 for each nine holes. Entertainer Phil Harris, who still lives there, bought the first home building lot on Thunderbird's 6,750-yard, par-72 course. Bing Crosby and Bob Hope soon followed. Thunderbird was one of the first clubs in

For almost 60 years, the biggest attraction to Palm Springs and the rest of the desert resort area has been golf. The lush Palm Valley Country Club course is one of many developed in recent years by the Sunrise Company.

the country to have home lots on fairways. Original lots sold for $2,000 each. The following year, the first $5,000 pro-am tournament in the valley was held at Thunderbird.

Tamarisk, Indian Wells, El Dorado, Bermuda Dunes and Palm Springs Country Clubs sprang up following the success of Thunderbird, where the first Bob Hope Classic was hosted in 1960. This world-renowned tournament has raised more than $18 million for charity over the years.

Soon, golf courses and country clubs began popping up across the valley: Morningside, Canyon, Vintage, Cathedral Canyon, P.G.A. West and The Springs were among the leaders. Today, from Palm Springs to Indio, there are verdant fairways and lush greens that form nearly a full valley carpet.

Each year golf enthusiasts await the Bob Hope Chrysler Classic, Nabisco-Dinah Shore, Frank Sinatra Celebrity and Vintage

Chrysler invitationals. And the PGA West's Stadium Course, the toughest in the country, annually hosts the high-stakes, four-player, "Skins" game.

TENNIS From grand stadiums to small city parks, there are more than 600 tennis courts in the desert resort area to tempt everyone. Since The Desert Inn installed the first court and was quickly followed by El Mirador, valley tennis courts have attracted from tyros to international-level players from all over the world.

Charlie Farrell's Racquet Club alone probably did as much as anything to propel the "sport of strings" to prominence in the valley. "During the 1970s," Bogert related in *Palm Springs—The First One Hundred Years*, "when tennis was on the rise in the United States, every hotel, country

The Hyatt Grand Champions Resort in Indian Wells hosts the Newsweek Champions Tennis Cup tournament each year at its 10,500-seat stadium.

club, condominium and many private homes built courts...The Davis Cup Tournament was played at the Racquet Club; other tournaments were staged at courts all over the city. For a while, tennis almost equaled golf in popularity."

Over the decades, tens of thousands have come to the valley for private or group instructions in tennis. Each year, the top men's professional tennis players compete in the Newsweek Champions Cup, a tournament held at the 10,500-seat stadium at Hyatt Grand Champions Resort in Indian Wells. Now in its 14th year (and earlier called the Pilot-Pen Cup), this $1 million event is one of only four on the Association of Tennis Professionals Tour held in the United States and one of eleven for touring pros worldwide.

POLO & RIDING
Since its early settlement days the desert resort area has held a fascination for horseback riding. One of the community's first major events was the annual trek of The Desert Riders, a group of local riders who each year spent many days riding into the nearby mountains and canyons.

As early as the 1920s this evolved into morning and moonlight rides from Smoke Tree Stables, where riding horses are still available today. Soon after, polo matches began. "Nowhere is polo more popular for the average spectator than in Southern California," according to Alexander Haagen III, owner of the new Empire Polo Club in Indio. Next door to Empire is the Eldorado Polo Club, where Britain's Prince Philip played a match called "The Duke of Edinburgh Award for Young People" a few years ago.

From late fall through spring of each year matches are played most Sundays at Eldorado. With seven tournament fields, 125 players and up to 1,000 ponies, Eldorado is known as the "Winter Polo Capital of the West."

For those less energetic in their equestrian interests, riding horses, with or without guides, can be found at Smoke Tree Stables in Palm Springs. From here, riding is available on an hourly or daily basis into the desert, mountains or Indian Canyons.

COURTESY PALM
SPRINGS ANGELS

ATTRACTIONS

PALM SPRINGS AERIAL TRAMWAY
Soaring more than 8,500 feet up the rugged Chino Canyon wall of the San Jacinto Mountain, the steepest rock face in the United States, the Aerial Tramway thrills more than 400,000 guests each year.

First opened a quarter-century ago, the world's most spectacular tram-

Since 1986, the Palm Springs Angels have entertained fans at more than 70 home games in the local stadium each year.

way has carried more than 7.5 million riders from the arid desert floor to the 54 miles of pristine and, in winter, snow-covered, trails at the summit wilderness. In summer, mule train rides are available. The 18-minute trip in dual 80-passenger gondolas takes visitors up two and one-half miles through five climatic life zones. In winter, when snow conditions permit, sled dog races are scheduled from the Tram top over a 2.5-mile course.

OASIS WATER PARK

Opened in 1986, the 21-acre Oasis Water Park in Palm Springs couldn't have a more appropriate name. With a one-acre wave-pool, the largest in California, and seven waterslides, including free-fall and twister slides up to 70-feet high, the water park offers something for all ages. For little ones there is a play area called "Squirt City." For the active, a pair of beach sand volleyball courts. To relax, a 600-foot "Whitewater River" inner tube ride, semi-private cabanas and a health club are available.

PALM SPRINGS ANGELS

A professional Class-A farm-club of the California Angels Baseball Club, the Palm Springs Angels schedule some 72 home games in the April to August season. The California Angels, owned by Gene Autry, play spring exhibition games in Palm Springs Angels Stadium. Paid attendance for the local team reached almost 73,000 last year.

SHALIMAR SPORTS CENTER

Located on the Date Festival grounds in Indio, the Shalimar Sports Center brings off-track horse race wagering

An 18-minute trip on the Palm Springs Aerial Tramway takes visitors up two and a half miles through five climatic life zones.

103

In the heart of Palm

Springs, the Village Green

Heritage Center preserves

Judge McCallum's adobe

home and Miss Cornelia

White's railroad-tie house.

to the valley. The center's "Watch and Wager" system, by way of pari-mutuel satellite, carries races run at Southern California tracks, as well as national events such as the Kentucky Derby. In its first year of operation, the soon-to-be-expanded facility handled almost $50 million in wagers from 110,000 race fans.

INSTITUTE OF GOLF

A new 5,000-square-foot clubhouse-styled operations center recently opened at the Institute of Golf at College of the Desert in Palm Desert. Its night-lighted driving range, pro shop and golf museum are open seven days a week to instruct everyone from kids to seniors. More than 100,000 people utilized this comparatively inexpensive resource last year.

VILLAGE GREEN HERITAGE CENTER

On South Palm Canyon, in the heart of Palm Springs, the Village Green Heritage Center is made up of two true pioneer houses and a quaint general store.

The McCallum Adobe, built in 1885 by the area's first white settler, John Guthrie McCallum, now is home to the Palm Springs Historical Society. Exhibits of photography, paintings, clothes, tools, books and Indian works from the city's first days are on display.

Miss Cornelia White's House was built with discarded railroad ties in 1894. Originally part of the first Palm Springs Hotel, purchased by "Miss Cornelia" in 1912, the house was moved across the street and she lived there until her death in 1961.

Ruddy's General Store, the third structure on the Village Green, lets visitors view a unique collection of showcases, signs, clothing and products in a re-created store from the 1930-1940 era.

The Mexican stone fountain at the Village Green Heritage Center was installed as part of the city's golden anniversary celebration in 1988. It is surrounded by sidewalk bricks carrying the names of donors.

LIVING DESERT

A 1,200-acre ethno-botanical reserve on the south side of Palm Desert, the Living Desert is one of the area's most popular tourist stops. At the foot of the Santa Rosa Mountains, this center has six miles of trails winding through eight different desert habitats, allowing plants and animals alike to live in natural surroundings. It features a nocturnal exhibit of live native mammals and reptiles. Bighorn sheep, slenderhorn gazelles and Arabian oryx roam the complex that was begun in 1969.

Above: In downtown Palm Springs, the Village Green Heritage Center recalls the area's earlier era.
Facing page: Begun 20 years ago, the Living Desert is a 1,200-acre refuge with six miles of nature trails. Located on the southern end of Palm Desert, the reserve also has more strenuous mountainside trails for the hardier tourist.

NATIONAL DATE FESTIVAL

Each February, with the date harvest well underway, Indio celebrates the Riverside County National Date Festival. The 10-day event begun in 1921 annually draws a quarter million people. Each evening guests are treated to an Arabian Nights Pageant produced on an outdoor stage, a reproduction of an ancient Baghdad market. By day, camel and ostrich races, clowns, mimes and daredevil acts enthrall young and old alike.

McCALLUM THEATER

A $20 million world-class complex, the McCallum Theater for the Performing Arts at the Bob Hope Cultural Center had its grand opening in 1988. Situated on 16 acres of land leased from College of the Desert, the 1,166-seat theater serves the desert resort area as a center for musicals, dance and entertainers, as well as college productions and public events. From classic to cowboy and drum corps to drama, this unique arts center hosts them all.

LA QUINTA ARTS FESTIVAL

Sixteen thousand art lovers spent some $400,000 at a recent La Quinta Arts Festival. For more than six years, this event, featuring the work of some 150 artists and craftspeople, has established itself as one of the nation's 10 top outdoor art festivals. Paintings, photography, sculpture and more are on display in a park-like setting at the foot of the Santa Rosa Mountains in the La Quinta cove each March.

Art interest in the Valley is fueled by dual sources. The 60 or more local galleries are supported half by tourists with the leisure time to browse, and half by the need to decorate the burgeoning number of hotels, homes and condominiums in the desert resort area.

Centerpiece of the Bob Hope Cultural Center in Palm Desert is the McCallum Theater for the Performing Arts.

From Arabian Nights at the

Date Festival to arts and

crafts at the La Quinta Arts

Festival, the Valley always

has something going.

Above: At the Aerie Sculpture Garden, Palm Desert.
Right: *Since 1921, Indio has been the location of the National Date Festival, which attracts 250,000 people annually.*

MUSEUMS & GARDENS

PALM SPRINGS DESERT MUSEUM

On a 20-acre site behind the Desert Fashion Plaza, the Palm Springs Desert Museum opened in 1976. The privately funded art and natural science center fills a 75,000-square-foot, split-level structure housing galleries, fountains, sunken sculpture gardens and a 450-seat theater for the performing arts. A continually changing exhibit program brings works by leading artists. In its natural sciences section, the museum displays nearly 1,300 American Indian artifacts, including some of the best examples of rugs and basketry.

MOORTEN'S BOTANICAL GARDENS   More than 2,000 varieties
of desert plants are on display at Moorten's Botanical Garden in Palm Springs. Hundreds of cactus varieties are showcased in an enclosed "cactarium." These are cultivated for and distributed to botanical outlets and museums world-wide. Arranged by geographical regions, the gardens have examples of desert plants from several continents. Visitors can also examine petrified logs, pioneer relics and sculpted wood and rock formations. The Moortens' "earthquake-proof" home is located in the garden area. Made of poured concrete over two miles of steel beams, the 60-year-old "Desertland" structure is an historic landmark.

CABOT'S OLD INDIAN PUEBLO MUSEUM   Cabot Yerxa, a
world-wanderer, homesteaded 160 acres of land in Desert Hot Springs in 1913. He spent 20 years building a Hopi Indian-style structure with 35 rooms, 150 windows and 65 doors. Today, this strange structure, an historic landmark, on East Desert View Avenue is a trading post and museum containing Indian relics, a rock shop and Pueblo Art Gallery.

GENERAL PATTON MEMORIAL MUSEUM   At exactly 11:00 a.m.
on November 11, 1988, a lone military jet screamed across the desert 30 miles east of Indio, marking the dedication of the General Patton Memorial Museum at Chiriaco Summit.

Patton, a four-star general and controversial hero of World War II, had headquarters for his 18,000-square-mile Desert Training Center at this site—the largest military installation and maneuver area in the world.

Today, a 7,000-square-foot center displays items from "Old Blood and Guts" Patton's life and career. A 17-foot statue of General Patton, who died in 1945, is to be displayed beside a World War II M-47 "Patton" tank.

Right: *In addition to museums and gardens, numerous city parks can be found across the valley. At a centennial event in a Palm Springs park, children were treated to elephant rides.*

Facing page, top: *Patricia Moorten at Moorten's Botanical Gardens.*
Bottom: *Cabot Yerxa thought Palm Springs too crowded when he arrived in 1913. He felt 107 neighbors were more than he needed. On a homestead plot north of the village he began to built his retreat. Today it is known as Cabot's Old Indian Pueblo Museum.*

GEORGE SERVICE PHOTOS
BOTH PAGES

NATURAL WONDERS

PALM SPRINGS INDIAN CANYONS
Open to visitors each year from September through June, the Palm Springs Indian Canyons offer hiking, horseback riding and picnic areas to more than 250,000 visitors yearly.

Carefully preserved by the Agua Caliente Band of Cahuilla Indians, these canyons are recognized as nature preserves. Reached through a tollgate at the end of South Palm Canyon Drive in Palm Springs, the Palm, Andreas and Murray canyons are a refuge for endangered birds and are listed in the National Register of Historic Places. Tahquitz Canyon, closer to the city, can be visited with special permits from the Tribal Council.

COACHELLA VALLEY PRESERVE
On the north side of Interstate 10, near Thousand Palms, the 13,000-acre Coachella Valley Preserve was established primarily to protect the endangered fringe-toed lizard. It is an unusual marriage of desert and aquatic habitats encompassing one of the largest groves of Washingtonia palm trees in California. Earth fractures caused by the infamous San Andreas Fault allow water to seep to the surface, sustaining the preserve's plant and animal life. A half-mile, self-guided trail lets visitors see what life was like in the desert area before golf courses were invented.

ANZA-BORREGO STATE PARK
This 600,000-acre state park, the largest in the California system, covers one fifth of San Diego County, as well as parts of Riverside and Imperial counties. South of the Coachella Valley and west of the Salton Sea, this strange land has elevations ranging from 500 to 6,000 feet.

Secluded canyons, jagged mountains and a wide array of wildlife can be found throughout the park. Bobcat, coyote and deer—and even the elusive bighorn sheep—can be found here. The intimidating landscape of the Borrego Badlands was formed by flash-floods, causing steep gullies, sharp ridges and deep valleys.

For additional information on these and other locations, contact the Palm Springs Desert Resorts Convention and Visitors Bureau, Suite 315, 255 N. El Cielo Road, Palm Springs, CA 92262, phone (619) 327-8411.

Above left: Sparrow hawk at Living Desert in Palm Desert.
Facing page: Joshua tree in Joshua Tree National Monument.

Endless sunshine, clean, dry air and a

wide range of activities await the arrival of

the more than 4 million people who are

welcomed yearly to the desert resorts.

At Shadow Mountain Resort, Palm Desert.